The Freedom Figure

How to Work Less, Live More, and Thrive in the
New World of Work

by

Adam Fletcher

Part 1 - Understand.

"If you always do what you've always done, you'll always get what you've always got." – Henry Ford

Chapter 1 - Everything Is Just Great, Isn't It?

Welcome, dear reader. You've picked a truly wonderful time in human history in which to join us. Very astute of you, if we may say so ourselves. You've deftly avoided *trephining, woolly mammoths, tunic wear, the plague, the world wars,* and *outside toilets,* to arrive at the tail end of 50 years of extravagantly calm technological and societal progress. Good job!

Yes, it really is a glorious time to be alive. Industrious humans have been busy upgrading your science, paving your roads, insulating your home, waterproofing your jacket, unionising your job, and arming your police force. We've even educated almost all of your neighbours. In fact, so many of life's necessities are already in place that we've even had some bonus time to develop largely unnecessary luxuries for your enjoyment—luxuries like the *lemon hat* (it helps keep your half lemons fresh), the *two-person umbrella* (wider and angled in the middle to support multi-person umbrella usage), the *E-cigarette* (like old cigarettes, but without the nasty smell, and even usable on a plane), and even the *heated towel rail* (warm strips of metal that help dry your towels in record time).

Because of all of this hard-fought-for innovation (especially the lemon hat), you are, statistically, predicted to live longer than at any point in human history, to the ripe old age of 78 (assuming you're a European man—83 if you had the foresight to be a woman). Because of our state-run education programs, you'll die smarter, more experienced, and having traversed more of our happy little globe than any of your ancestors would even have dared to dream. In fact, the technology you have at your daily disposal would be sufficient to convince your ancestors that you are a God. They would be amazed by someone who could point squares of plastic into the sky and communicate directly with the heavens. You will call it *googling,* it will mean nothing to you.

You can access all this knowledge while on the move because of something called *the smartphone*, a pocket-sized communications ninja that you can take out and point at the sky to ask pertinent questions, or just be shown funny cat videos. Whatever your whim or need for distraction, there is a €0.99 app being built to service it. Your smartphone already contains more raw processing power than NASA used to put man on the moon back in 1969. Did I mention we've already visited the moon? Yep. I'm sure you'll be heading there on holiday soon enough. Don't forget your lemon hat.

Since you still have basic physical needs like love and procreation, we've done our best to widen your potential dating pool. Your forefathers and sisters were often born, came of age, dated, married, had children, and died within a hundred kilometers of their birthplace, having picked just one solitary mate that had to last them a lifetime, like some sort of swan. *Idiots*.

You? Well, you get to pick from a far larger human orchard. There's a dating website for every imaginable niche, and marriage has never been less popular. *Today* is the new *forever*. Play the field. Make mistakes. Swipe left for no, right for yes. Feel free to kiss a lot of frogs in the pursuit of your ~~prince/cess~~ next life-phase partner.

Your work options have also matured. We've evolved out of—or outsourced away from—all that undignified hitting-things-with-other-things nonsense. Instead, in its place is a whole raft of *brain work* now available to you, should you choose to study for it. Often, you can even interface remotely with work from the familiar warmth of your home. Or you can create a simple Internet business and become your own boss, selling your services to anyone on the planet who might require them. Today, starting an international company is almost as easy as starting a local one, for the Internet neither respects nor acknowledges borders.

If, despite all this abundance, you get bored of everything we've built and are able to enjoy, feel free to just rip it up, hop on a plane, and start an entirely new life tomorrow, somewhere warmer, completely reinventing yourself in the process. Apparently Thailand is nice this time of year.

Yes, living today is like arriving in the middle of a great party—a never-ending, all-you-can-eat riot of technological wizardry and human ingenuity...right? Right!

So, knowing all this, who would be so brazen, so foolish, so contrarian as to look at all of this shiny plug-and-play progress and *dare* to be critical? To suggest that, beneath the surface, there are serious and fundamental problems with the structure of society? With inequality? With resource distribution? With the intergenerational contract? And that these problems are being ever-accelerated by the speed of technological progress? That, for today's younger generations, this might not be such a golden time of prosperity after all? That if life today is a party, it's actually a party that is past its peak?

Well, I would...

A young man asks an older, richer man how he made his money. The old gentleman fingers his expensive tweed coat and says:

"Well son, it was 1931. The depths of the Depression. I was down to my last penny. I invested that penny in an apple. I spent the entire day polishing that apple, and, at the end of the day, I sold that apple for two pennies.

"The next morning, I invested those two pennies in two apples. I spent the entire day polishing them and then sold them for four pence. I continued this system of polishing and selling, each time reinvesting my profits into buying more apples."

"Wow!" says the young man, "and that's how you accumulated your fortune?"

"Nah," replies the old man, "my wife's father died and left us a million pounds."

Chapter 2 - No, Actually It Isn't

Arriving at the digital party of today, the first thing you notice is that it's gotten rather crowded. Removing your shoes, you enter and look around nervously for someone you might know. Unable to find someone, you squeeze into the kitchen to look for a drink, only to discover it's also gotten mightily congested. Peering over the shoulders of several million strangers, you see that the buffet's been ransacked, vodka bottles lay empty on their side, and tempers are beginning to fray. You'd like to find a nice place to sit down and rest, but several billion people appear to have beaten you to that, as well, and the seats are all gone in what was a heavily contested global game of musical chairs. Now, the few chairs that remain have gotten very expensive, and a long queue has formed to take out a mortgage for one, which you appear to be at the very asset-less back of. *Darn.*

Stumbling around in confusion, you head to where most of the people are, in the center of things. There, you spot a middle-aged man in a dark corner who has several chairs all to himself, yet appears only to have *one* ass. You sidle up next to him and nod at one of his vacant seats. "Any chance we could sit there, buddy?"

"That's mine," he says.

"Yes, but you're not using it right now, are you?"

"It's my second chair," he says, proudly.

"You need a second chair?"

"Yes."

"Why?"

"This one," he says, nodding down at the empty chair, "faces outside, and has a view of the park." As if to demonstrate this perk, he moves across and sits on it, craning his neck towards a nearby window, which does, indeed, look out to a largely uninspiring view of a single tree. "I sit here on weekends sometimes, when I want to get away from the main throb of the party. It's very relaxing."

"Okay, then what about that chair?" you ask, pointing at a slightly dilapidated third chair a meter or so away. This third chair faces neither the park nor the party—just a bare white wall.

"You mean my third chair?" the man replies.

"Yes. Can I sit on that?"

"Unfortunately, not. That's my *buy-to-let* chair. It's in a very up-and-coming chair area. I'm going to rent that chair out."

"I'd just like to sit there for a little while. If that's okay? If someone else wants it, I'll gladly move."

Mr. Three-Chairs rolls his eyes. "I've worked hard for all my chairs. Why do you young people think you should get everything for free? Always bumming around, taking your selfies and looking for a handout. You can rent the chair if you like. For just €600 a month, plus three months rent as a deposit, €45 cushion security fee, and €65 for a credit reference."

"That seems like a lot," you say, turning out your pockets to find them completely empty.

"Like I said, it's an up-and-coming chair area. I couldn't rent it cheaper to my own mother. Not that she needs another chair. Actually, she gave me that chair."

"Okay, I understand, sir. But the problem is, I've just arrived, and so don't have any money yet."

"Find a job, then. Do you have skills? Talk to the people running around in white dinner jackets, they might have a job for you," says the man, gesturing back over your shoulder.

Turning around, you spot a woman in a white dinner jacket, carrying a tray of drinks. She looks sad but industrious, focusing on traversing the room without spilling anything. You approach her and smile.

"Hello, madam. I was hoping you might have a job for me?"

The lady looks you up and down, as if checking for any visible flaws. "A job, you say? Well, isn't everyone? What with the economy and all. Yes, difficult time, isn't it? Not much going around, I'm afraid. You know, with the economy being what it is and all." She shakes her head and looks down to her feet. "Yes, difficult. Do you have relevant experience?"

"No. But I'm a fast learner. Also, I have a degree. I just graduated, in fact."

The woman pulls a face like she's being stung by a thousand invisible wasps. "No relevant experience then." She pauses, thinking. "I could offer you a job as *apprentice-trainee-junior-assistant-beverage-dispensation-coordination-supervisor.* It's an internship. There's no pay, but after six months you'll have experience and contacts, and there's a very good chance of a permanent, paid *apprentice-trainee-junior-assistant-beverage-dispensation-coordination-supervisor* position."

Success! "Okay, and what would that pay?" you ask. "Minimum wage," is the deadpan response.

You're not exactly sure what we're worth, but you're sure it's more than that. So, you head back towards the exit, squeezing careful between bodies, apologising for always being in the way. You reach where you felt sure the door was. But then, looking down for the handle, there is nothing. No handle. No door. Just a white wall. You turn around in circles a few times, pulse rising. Maybe you're mistaken? "Hello, does anyone know where the way out is?" you shout. "Where's the exit?!"

"HELLO?" you shout again, louder and with more urgency. No one answers. The music continues to throb. Looking down, another zero has been added to your bill.

Chapter 3 – What Happened?

Many people will say that the problems we have now—the loss of middle class jobs, the gig economy, youth unemployment, rising domestic inequality, the economic recession of the past years—are just a blip. They'll say that they're a fallout from a recent economic crisis triggered by the sale and resale of long-camouflaged toxic debts. The youth and middle class might be struggling now, but once the economy picks up, they will return with a minivan buying, foreign holiday enjoying, procreating, consuming vengeance.

The system? The system is fine. We don't need to change how our lives are structured. We can just do what our parents did. All will be fine.

This isn't true. The system is not fine. This is not a blip. It's an inevitability of our economy as it currently operates. It's the conclusion of a long-ago written story stretching all the way back to the Industrial Revolution.

Therefore, in order to understand where we are today—how society and employment are likely to develop in the future, and why it's important that we build our lives in a different way to make us less dependent on the state and our employers—we need to understand the system's underlying problems. Let's go back to the beginning...

I'll Work for ~~Me~~ You

Before the Industrial Revolution, life was particularly hard. Simple things like a cold, fever, or paper cut could quickly escalate and kill us, *dead*. If we lived to 40 we were considered one of the lucky ones, especially if we filled those 40 years having regularly gotten to do fun things like eating and washing ourselves. Life was simpler then. Most people were farmers and had plots of land, so they worked for themselves, growing things to eat or tending animals. If not, they likely had a specific trade like those of the carpenter or blacksmith, working away each day in small workshops, sawing and bashing things into useful shapes.

Then, thanks to the technical wizardry of the Industrial Revolution, people began to work out far smarter ways to grow, process, and bash *many things* all at once, using machines. Machines were like people, only less fickle and so not in need of gossip or tea breaks. So, over time, the people of the farms and workshops were offered work in factories, interacting with and supervising machines. These factories were, in effect, giant tool sheds that their employers unlocked for them each morning and locked again each night. In these tool sheds, employees did things with the employers' tools and machinery, and then every hour their employers paid them for the things they did. The employers then sold these things on for a profit for themselves.

People called it a *job*. It was an excellent way to fill the day.

With the seductive promise of a regular paycheck and working hours, less and less of us chose to work for ourselves, and instead became employees. The single largest employment migration of all time began. We lent these companies our time, willingness, and expertise. They promised to return to us a respectable career, an income that would lift us out of poverty, and a chance to own a home in which we could create a family—the sort of family who would enthusiastically welcome us home each night when we walked in for dinner, grubby and tired from a day's hard labour.

It made sense for these businesses, since they now had a reliable labour pool that would stream into their factories at agreed upon times (possibly earlier than that labour might have found desirable). With this labour pool assured, the businesses had greater certainty, meaning they could fulfill larger and larger contracts for the products they made, which in turn meant they could buy bigger and more expensive machines, producing more units for less money in a shorter period of time, to be sold to more people through the realisation of the economies that come with *scale*. Scale was good. Bigger was better. Productivity skyrocketed.

"In 1912, 4664 worker-hours were required to build a car. By the mid 1920s, one could be built in less than 813 worker-hours...Between 1920 and 1927, productivity in American industry rose by 40%. In manufacturing, output per man-hour rose by an astounding 5.6% a year between 1919 and 1929," says Jeremy Rifkin in his book *The End of Work.*[1]

Trades—collections of related skills like carpentry, baking, and blacksmithing that were traditionally passed down in a family from one generation to the next and were highly specialised, often taking years to master—underwent systematic simplification under the stopwatch of Taylorism and its ambassadors. Skills and trades could be sliced ever more thinly, and so learned more quickly and "on the job" by just about anyone with the arms, legs, and willingness to do so. We began swapping a depth of knowledge in our chosen craft, handed down from our fathers and mothers, for breadth. *Simple. Repeatable. Trackable.*

From Job to Career

Of course, these businesses did not work in isolation. They relied on other businesses, like wholesalers and distributors to get their products out from the gates of the factory into the eager hands of their customers. So a light bulb factory would often have the raw materials supplier for its glass just down the road, or a distributor for its light bulbs located a short drive away. It made economic sense for these businesses to cluster themselves near other related businesses, infrastructure, and potential employees.

Slowly, towns grew up to become cities, set to a soundtrack of hammers, prosperity, and nearly flawless GDP growth (if we ignore a few war-shaped blips).

All this commerce and capitalism needed both a stern referee and a zealous tax collector—the *government*. Governments sat above these businesses and (in theory) regulated them, working to make society better and fairer. Governments would educate the citizens that would become the employees of the future, in schools. Each time companies treated us badly (or at least after sufficient protest from us), governments blew their whistles and gave out fines and changed laws to make them stricter. Like bureaucratic superheroes, they promised to protect us from the free market's sharper edges. Since they'd set the rules of the game, and from birth we were essentially forced to play, they'd at least do us the favour of trying to keep it as fair as possible so we'd have the best chance of winning. We paid governments for their supervision by giving them a little of our wages, in the form of taxes. Also, because otherwise they might put us in jail.

In turn, these governments made certain promises to us. Those savings in our bank accounts? They would be safe. They would guarantee those for us. If we had trouble finding a job, they'd take some cash from society's collective piggy bank and support us until we got back on our feet. What's that down by our feet? Some trash? Hand it over then. Getting old, citizen? Don't worry about that—the government will pay for you to have a comfortable, relaxing few years of light gardening and watching snooker, with something called a *pension*. Governments promised to supervise the tedious, administrative parts of our existence so that we'd have time to focus on the things that really interested us, like drinking scotch, reading the newspaper, and coveting our neighbour's wives.

With economic certainty for both the employee and employer, things changed for the better. We suddenly had masses of the population regularly working and earning money, day after day, month after month, year after year. So the factories had far more people to which they could sell the things they'd spent all day making. The hourly wage became the yearly salary. With it, we employees had the certainty required to make larger financial bets of our own. There was no reason to believe life would be any worse or that we'd be any poorer tomorrow or in 10 years. So we felt assured enough to take out mortgages to buy our homes, or debt to send our children off to university.

We needed these university qualifications because machines kept increasing in complexity—as did people and collections of people (know as *teams* and *unions*),who needed ever more sophisticated supervision, by, you guessed it, yet more people. Universities were places where we could learn the skills required for all these newer, higher aptitude jobs. Maybe we had to pay a little something, but it was an *investment*. An investment in our future. A future of ever-increasing length, thanks to advances in sanitation, health, and medical care, which saw life expectancy rising dramatically. Employment was still high, and we could practically be assured that on the final day of our studies we'd step out of university and quickly into a respectable career. Yep, not a *job*, but a *career*.

The nature of what we'd do at these companies would probably change over time, but it was still entirely feasible that we'd pick just one company and work there our entire adult working lives, culminating in nervous speeches to our colleagues, some cake, and engraved clocks for our mantelpieces.

The Wheels Fall off the Wagon

There were two important variables working throughout all of this happy progress—*employment* and *productivity*.

"Productivity is the amount of economic value that is generated for a given unit of input, such as an hour of labour—it is a crucial indicator of growth and wealth creation.[2]" Employment is the amount of humans it takes to achieve this level of productivity.

Employment is important, because the output of all that productivity is usually a product/service that needs to be sold to someone to pay back the costs incurred in producing it. Humans that are employed tend to have the money to buy things being produced. They are not only *producers*, but *consumers*. Their consumption creates further demand, and so logically further production, and yet further employment, and so on. As one increases, so should the other. This is exactly what happened throughout the twentieth century. Below you can find US manufacturing output since 1918, showing a remarkable increase in productivity over the previous hundred years.

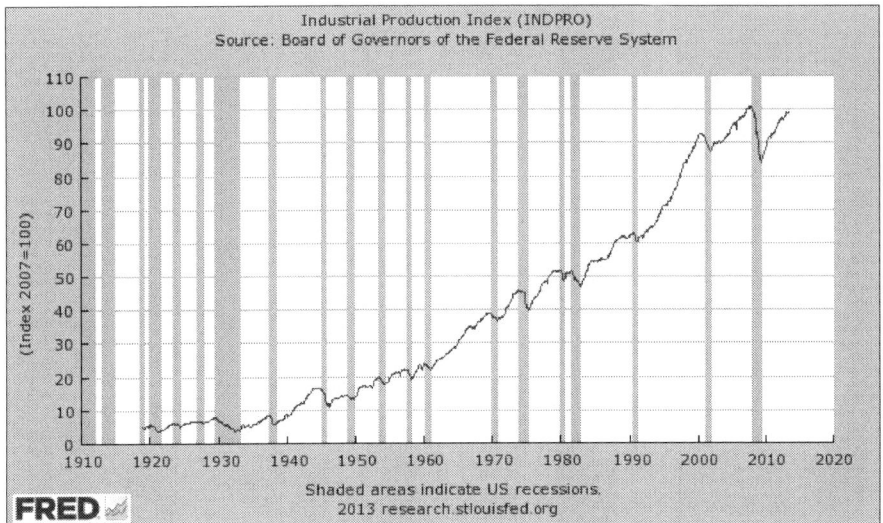

Industrial Production Index (INDPRO)
Source: Board of Governors of the Federal Reserve System
Shaded areas indicate US recessions.
2013 research.stlouisfed.org

3

Now, let's take a look at how many humans were needed to create all that productivity. Again, over the same time period in the US.

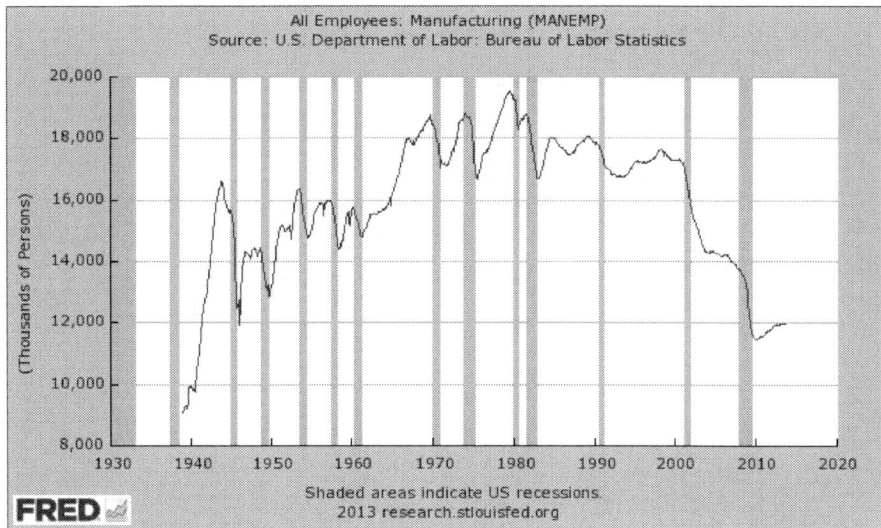

All Employees: Manufacturing (MANEMP)
Source: U.S. Department of Labor: Bureau of Labor Statistics

Shaded areas indicate US recessions.
2013 research.stlouisfed.org

4

Oh, that's not quite what we expected, right?

US manufacturing employment peaked in 1980, and has been rapidly declining ever since. Nor is it just in the US. "Some 22 million manufacturing jobs were lost globally between 1995 and 2002 as industrial output soared 30 percent.[5]"

We're producing more, but we need far less people to do that. "Since 1978, manufacturing employment has declined by about 40%. Over the same period of time, the U.S. population has grown by about 40%. As a percentage of a much larger workforce, the percent of U.S. workers in manufacturing has declined by more than half.[6]"

Declines like this are okay if people have somewhere else to retrain into, and ample time to retrain. This time, most retrained into services, a sector now also being automated at a rapid rate.
Nothing about this displacement of humans via technology is new. It's been happening repeatedly since the Industrial Revolution, and probably far earlier still. What is new, however, is the speed of this displacement. This is because of something called The Law of

18

Accelerating Returns.

More Change, More Often

The Law of Accelerating Returns dictates that not only are things changing ever more quickly, but that the time between those significant changes is also reducing. In short: more change, more often. It's a term coined by Ray Kurzweil, who believes: "We won't experience 100 years of progress in the 21st century—it will be more like 20,000 years of progress (at today's rate)...There's even exponential growth in the rate of exponential growth.[7]"

This is because each breakthrough benefits from all previous breakthroughs, which explains why human life expectancy has increased more in the last 50 years than in the previous 200,000 years of human existence[8]. Each new technology builds on top of all the possibilities combined from every technology it supersedes. The airplane can only exist because someone invented the combustion engine. The combustion engine can only exist because some bright spark learned to mine steel and oil. It took thousands of years for even the most basic of inventions like fire or the wheel to reach mass adoption, as primitive man lugged his knuckles around trying really hard just to find enough food to stay alive. Just as it was hard for him to wrap his head around the wheel or a simple stone tool, it's hard for us to wrap our heads around something as intangible as exponential growth, which is how we experience change.

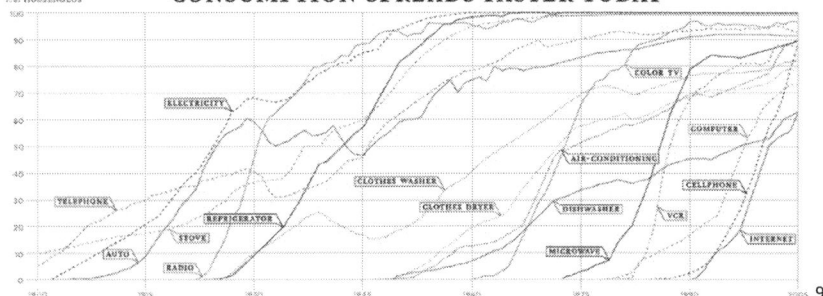

Where Does That Leave Us?

Humans solve problems and sell their solutions for money. It has always been this way, and it will always be this way. It's annoying to get up and change the TV channel, so someone invented the remote control. "It's hot" leads to the air conditioner. We like massages and we like sitting, so we invent the massage chair. But then it's only logical to assume that, at some point, *we* might become the very problem that our solutions are sent out to solve—that somewhere in a corner office, looking out through glass at a production line, at a restaurant floor full of bussing waiters and waitresses, at a newsroom of journalists and researchers—a disruptive new technology is turning to its creator and saying, *"You see those people out there that you have to pay each month, boss? With their mood swings? Their holiday requests? Their petty problems and politics? Their parental leave? Can I help you with that? We don't really need them. Your shareholders will thank me."*

Horst Neumann, chief of human resources for Volkswagen, Germany's bigger car manufacturer, explained the cost savings of adopting this new technology in place of human labour. "In the German auto industry, labour costs are more than €40 per hour, Eastern European labour costs €11, in China, it's still less than €10…A current robotic replacement for assembly work currently costs around €5 an hour. Predictably, next generation robotics will

20

be even cheaper. We have to make the most of this price advantage.[10]"

"We are now entering the beginning of an era in which technology has started to destroy employment faster than it creates it. The advance of information technology, artificial intelligence, and robotics will eventually reduce the demand for all forms of human labor…" believes James Hughes, a sociologist from Trinity College in Connecticut.[11]

Rather than science fiction, this is already an everyday feature of our lives. "Software is picking out worrisome blots in medical scans, running trains without conductors, driving cars without drivers, spotting profits in stocks trades in milliseconds, analyzing Twitter traffic to tell where to sell certain snacks, sifting through documents for evidence in court cases, recording power usage beamed from digital utility meters at millions of homes, and sorting returned library books.[12]"

The process of humans losing their job to AI or robots is called *technological unemployment*. Opinions about its severity are still very much disputed. Many people believe it is not a problem at all—that it has always been a factor of life. The belief that there could be any kind of fixed amount of labour is merely a fallacy. Instead, new technology slowly automates away the simplest, cheapest jobs, and slowly pushes everyone upwards into better white-collar jobs doing new things made possible by that new technology. In the past, that might have been true. We certainly have less people toiling away in the fields today than 100 years ago, and that's to our collective betterment. However, it's possible the digital revolution will not behave like the Industrial Revolution. This time, the AI and machines are not just targeting low skills jobs, but *middle class* jobs, either replacing them entirely or breaking them down into lower skills jobs.

"The AI revolution is doing to white collar jobs what robotics did to blue collar jobs,[13]" believe Brynjolfsson and McAfee, authors of the book *Race Against the Machine*. These effects are already evident in the jobs market. "In the 17 European countries that use the euro as their currency...almost 4.3 million low-pay jobs have been gained since mid-2009, but the loss of mid-pay jobs has never stopped. A total of 7.6 million disappeared from January 2008 through last June.[14]" In Germany, the number of full-time workers on low pay increased by 13.5 percent to 4.3 million between 2005 and 2010, three times faster than other employment, according to the German Labour Office.[15] Those still in work have found themselves in less favourable negotiation positions, which might explain why real wage growth in Germany from 1992 to 2012 was just 0.6%.[16]

The Rise of Uncertainty

Each freshly released technology that we create, whether it's the Internet, the printer, email, the mobile phone, or Facebook, rushes straight out society's *barriers of the possible*, the fences that have held us back until that point, whether legal, moral, technical, or merely logistical. Then it throws itself against them, one by one, probing for a weakness. The Internet and all that it's enabled have turned out to be so powerful that they're smashing with reckless abandon through previously impenetrable fences that have protected institutions like university, employment, marriage, and even democracy itself, as well as the elastic band that's held all those together—government.

"Every new technology creates almost as many problems that it solves..." says Kevin Kelly, author of *What Technology Wants*. "One way to think about this is if you imagine the very first tool made, say, a stone hammer. That stone hammer could be used to kill somebody, or it could be used to make a structure, but before that stone hammer became a tool, the possibility of making that choice did not exist. Technology is continually giving us ways to do harm and to do well; it's amplifying both.[17]"

New technologies can be a force for good or bad. Alberto Santos-Dumont, the aviation pioneered, believed that the airplane would end all wars. It's hard to imagine what he might think of today's drone warfare.

Technology is not a silver bullet. It's not magically going to make life better. On the surface, rampant technological progress should be enabling and liberating us, and for many this is the case. However, technology does not exist in a vacuum. It is applied on top of a complicated cluster fuck of inefficient social structures. Social structures full of entrenched bureaucracy, unequal resource distribution, and intergenerational conflicts that we lovingly refer to as *society*. These are complicated, inefficient social structures that we often neither understand nor have the laws yet to control for the benefit of everyone. This helps to explain why, today, with so much new technology and so many smart people wielding it, we sometimes feel dizzy just trying to keep up with the rate of change. We're forced to react as best we can, players scrambling to stay good at a game that's forever having its rules rewritten in front of us.

This march of progress has been equally challenging for the businesses that employ us. On the plus side, they can reach customers more easily than ever before. However, so can their competitors. Those big expensive machines that had previously represented such a big part of their competitive advantage keep shrinking and getting less expensive. This makes them affordable for more people, which leads to more competition, which in turn can be located anywhere. Unable to accurately forecast demand far into the future, businesses are forced to pass that uncertainty on to us, their employees. As a result, unlimited contracts become limited contracts. Limited contracts became temp agency contracts. Temp contracts became zero-hour contracts. Full-time jobs become mini-jobs. Increasingly, there's a discrepancy between what we want (security) and what companies require of us (flexibility).

Today, the idea of "a job for life" is terribly quaint, like the horse and cart or the quill pen.

The Government of One

Another worrying development is that new generations of technology companies like Facebook and Google are not like previous companies. They transcend any physical location, existing only online. So why should they be loyal to one particular country? They can go wherever there are good staff and the right economic conditions for them flourish. Just as loyalty between employers and employees is breaking down, so, increasingly, are relations between companies and governments. Governments are left on the digital sideline, scratching their heads and trying to work out what is going on, what it is exactly that these companies are offering and, more importantly, *how they can tax some of it.*

Knowing that businesses are not tied by geography, and that they are willing to move if the conditions are right, governments of different countries have actually started to compete against each other to try and attract businesses to incorporate in their territory, under pressure from their citizens to create jobs. Plucky little nations like Ireland have offered massive tax breaks and free land to encourage tech companies like Google, HP, or Intel to relocate there. However, the more governments bid for the business of corporations, the less those same corporations have an incentive to be loyal to them—or to us, their employees. Once those favourable terms expire, they know another government somewhere is preparing an attractive package to try and win their business.

Reports suggest that Apple have created the world's largest *rainy day fund,* stashing some 10 billion dollars away in a tax haven where it can't be taxed for the benefit of any of the sovereign nations in which it was earned. *"Apple Inc. established an offshore subsidiary, Apple Operations International, which from 2009 to 2012 reported net income of $30 billion, but declined to declare any* *tax residence, filed no corporate income tax return, and paid no corporate income taxes to any national government for five years,"* says a recent US senate report on Apple's tax avoidance[18]. Google has a reported 33 billion dollars holed up in the tiny tax agnostic island of Bermuda.[19] The Bermuda triangle really does exist, but it's not planes that disappear there—it's other nations' tax money.

It's easy to dismiss that lost tax money as never really being ours—as belonging merely to our inept governments, unable to collect what is owed to them. But it belongs to us. It's owed to us, indirectly, via our governments. It's new super hospitals that we can't open. Funding for schools we can't open. State housing we can't build. Social support we can't offer.

It's tempting to get really angry about this. But just as we are trying to react to technological change and impermanence, so are our governments. Just as our time horizons are shrinking, so are theirs. Many might consider their behaviour deplorable, but it is also, at a certain level, understandable. The primary aim of any government is to get re-elected. The primary aim of a CEO is to raise the share price. The average tenure of a European CEO is around five years.[20] A head of state might be lucky enough to stay in power for 10. Their jobs—and consequently their foresight—have a built-in expiry date. The government and CEO of today does not answer to the generation of tomorrow—it answers only to the voters of its next election. So why should it think about that future generation? Why should it plan for the long term? Who will even remember in 15 years that you were once CEO? Will the firm even exist in 15 years? Who was chancellor 15 years ago? Better to bail out the influencers of today and ensure short-term prosperity, safe in the knowledge that you can always pass that debt on to future generations, long after it ceases to be your problem. It's not necessarily malicious, or corrupt, or even an example that capitalism is broken and we're all doomed. It's just people choosing self-preservation by any means possible, within the system as it is currently built.

Governments must also take into account that the more strongly they regulate, the greater the incentive to circumvent regulation. The stronger the tax laws are in Germany, the more businesses that will incorporate in Jersey or Bermuda. The stronger we make employment regulation to protect full-time employees, the more companies will hire freelancers or remote workers in countries with no such protections. The greater the rental protections in cities like London, Stockholm, or New York become, the larger the black market of illegal sublets will be. Finding the right balance is difficult. It's easy to end up having to run faster and faster, just to stand still. The more global the world becomes, the truer the cliché will be that *nobody wins unless everybody wins*.

As a result, we're in a race—to replace jobs as fast as technology obsoletes them, to update laws as fast as technology undermines them, to find new ways of governance and taxation faster than technology circumvents them, to keep taking prosperity from the few and returning it to the many. Sometimes we're winning, our economies grow, and there's something like stability for the masses. Other times, like the recession of the past five years, we're lagging far behind technological progress. There's a deficit, and that deficit is paid by the many on behalf of the few.

Case Study - Amazon.com

If you want an example of the kind of border-defying, job-destroying, technology-driven hyper-capitalism I've been talking about thus far, Amazon.com is pretty much perfect. Amazon encapsulates how one single company, while offering a service everyone wants, can circumvent and disintermediate a hundred others that people need, avoid paying tax, destroy more jobs than they create, and transition people from salaried to temporary work (largely bereft of any benefits), whilst still being viewed as a net positive by most of us.

Amazon - The art of Selling €11 for €10

The problem Amazon picked to solve is a simple one—shopping on the high street is annoying and largely inefficient for us (it even involves leaving the house!), and for the businesses that operate there (who have to pay high rents and staff costs). The solution Amazon sells is that everything you can buy on the high street can be delivered directly to your door within 48 hours (it'll probably be more like one hour for major cities by the time they finish, as is already being trialed with certain products in New York)—and for the same price or less as normal retail shopping.

Unfortunately, until now, the cost of providing this solution to us (the massive initial cost of creating the warehouses, IT systems, staffing, distribution, etc.) has been so prohibitively large that they've not been able to do so profitably without breaking a few rules. In effect, until now, they've been selling us €11 for €10 and charging our governments for the deficit. "In my world, [it's] not a real business. I get it if you don't make money for two or three years, but Amazon is, what, 21 years old?" said former Microsoft CEO Steve Ballmer in a recent interview.[21]

It works like this:

Step 1 - Incorporate in a tax haven.

In Europe, Amazon is registered in the tax haven of Luxembourg. Their businesses in the rest of Europe are labeled as "order fulfillment," which exempts them from paying corporation tax in those countries. This is despite the fact that Amazon has 7,000 full-time staff members in the UK[22] and 9,000 in Germany[23] (and around double as many temps, depending on the time of year), while its head office in Luxembourg, overseeing the whole of Europe, has just 800. As a result, in 2013, Amazon paid a reported €3m in German tax on sales of $8.7bn.[24] In the UK that same year, it actually received more in government grants to open warehouses than it paid in corporation tax, on UK sales of £4.2bn.[25] Amazon Europe Holding Technologies, it's partner firm in Luxembourg, did report a profit of €118m, but because of its tax-exempt status paid no income tax on it.[26]

Step 2 - Use cost savings from not paying tax to sell products at cheaper prices than your tax-paying competitors can offer.

Because they avoid paying VAT and have lower costs than high street stores, they can sell products for less, which makes them more attractive than local stores. Local stores can't compete, and end up going bust. However, every euro we spend in a local store has a chance of benefiting our local community.[27] Both the business where we spend that euro and the employee that we gave it to are taxed on their income by our local government, who use this euro to provide services to our local area—within the schools that educate our children, the roads we use to get them there, or myriad other local services like street lights, parks, garbage collection, etc., that make where we live a pleasant place to be. In contrast, if you spend this euro at Amazon, you are taking that euro from our local community and giving it to a company based in Luxembourg.

This is not an online versus offline debate, since there are many online businesses that both pay tax and reward their staff with permanent work contracts and benefits like sick pay and holiday.

Step 3 - Under pressure to create jobs, governments offer Amazon tax breaks to open offices/warehouses to replace the sorts of jobs lost to Amazon.

Just as Luxembourg bids for Amazon's business by offering lucrative tax terms, governments like the UK are offering Amazon subsidies to open warehouses in economically challenged areas (£8.8m in Swansea,[28] £2.5m in Dunfermline[29]), in the spirit of *job creation*. The irony of this is either lost on them, or they have a very dark sense of humour. In the words of Martin Smith of the GMB union, "They are taking these massive subsidies from the state and they are not paying back. Their argument is that they are creating jobs, but what they are doing is displacing and replacing other jobs. Better jobs. And high street shops tend to pay their taxes. There is a £120bn tax gap that is only possible because the government pay tax benefits to enable people to survive. When companies pay the minimum wage, they are in effect being subsidised by the taxpayer.[30]"

Step 4 - Employ these newly unemployed people, but with little job security or benefits, until you can find a way to automate them.

While Amazon employs staff, they need less per million in revenue than high street stores[31]. They also earn low wages (€9.55 in Germany,[32] €3.10 in Poland,[33] £7.39 in the UK), or Amazon benefits by "relying on employment agencies to hire temporary workers[34] whom Amazon can pay less, avoid paying them benefits, and fire them virtually at will" says Simon Head, author of *Mindless: Why Smarter Machines Are Making Dumber Humans[35]*. As a result, these staff member may require financial support from the government—which is paid for by tax revenue, of which there is now less, because it's gone to Luxembourg instead. In 2012, Amazon acquired robotics company Kiva Systems. It's already using 15,000 of its robots across 10 of its 50 US distribution centers.[36]

Step 5 - Reinvest profits back into larger infrastructure and further automation.

With your costs reducing as you scale, you can reinvest your money back into widening and automating your distribution network to get more items to more people within those 48 hours. Once you've enough scale, you'll be in a position to replace inefficient distribution methods like printed books with efficient ones like eBooks. Once you have less competition, you'll be able to raise prices.

Step 6 - Profit.

Rather than continuing to sell €11 for €10, you're now legitimately able to sell €5 for €10, since you've built the distribution network, eradicated most of your competitions, avoided as much tax as possible, and still receive government subsidies in the form of benefits paid to your staff members not receiving the livable wage.

Think of society like a leaking bucket. It can carry water. It's not perfect. We all see the water leaking out of the bottom—it gets our shoes wet. But it's the best bucket we've devised so far, and in it we do our best to keep as much water in as we can, for as long as we can. There are two ways we can improve it to hold more water: 1) fix the hole or 2) find a way to pour water in faster. Every time a local government takes tax money and gives it to Amazon to open a warehouse to create crappy jobs for the sorts of people who have already lost their jobs to Amazon, it's asking Amazon to flood our bucket with more water. It does nothing to fix the holes that we have, in which Amazon is more than complicit. At some point we're going to have to plug them. The question is if we all realise that, and find a way to do so before Amazon pours so much water in that the whole bucket collapses out from under our grip. Of course, we can change how society functions and close the loopholes businesses like Amazon or Google are using, but that takes a huge amount of time.

There are signs that we're making progress, however. A recent EU change to VAT law that came into effect on 1st January 2015 and stipulates that tax is paid at the customer's location, not the company's, closed a major loophole. In the UK, a so-called "Google Tax" has also just been announced. Companies deemed to be artificially offshoring their tax liabilities to tax havens like Luxembourg will be taxed 25% on them, regardless.

It's not that Amazon is in any way evil or particularly deserving of our vitriol. Nor is everyone having a job necessarily a good goal for society. We've out-evolved that. But it's how society functions now. Amazon is a fantastically useful company, doing nothing illegal. I'm a customer, and no doubt you are as well. They're the best at what they do. They're simply the smartest predator. If they weren't taking advantage of every competitive opportunity, their successor would be. In the same way that you probably wouldn't volunteer to pay a cent more tax than you really have to, it's no surprise that they won't either. They push to the very legal limits of what society allows, and it's all of our jobs (but mostly our governments') to make sure we stand together and push back—not an appeal to corporate morality, but from a firm commitment to robust legislation.

"Most of the problems we have today are technogenic, meaning that they were created by technology in the past. Most of the problems in the future are going to be created by technologies we're creating today. Technology is a means of producing new problems."

- Kevin Kelly, author of What Technology Wants

Chapter 4 - What can we do about it?

Rapid technological progress is affecting all areas of our lives. The world is changing more often and more drastically than at any point in human history thanks to Moore's Law and the Law of Accelerating Returns. Where our ancestors might have lived through one life-changing technology in a lifetime, we've already witnessed the introduction of the PC, the mobile phone, and the Internet. Contained within each are smaller revolutions of work— email, the spreadsheet—that require us to learn new skills, or automate away the old ones that previously kept us competitive in the job market (a job market offering less permanent and more temporary work).

As a result, the only certainty in our lives and is that there will be much, much more uncertainty. Either we wield technology and become its beneficiaries, or we have it wielded upon us and likely end up its victims. We'll be left chasing ever lower incomes in ever more temporary jobs, supported by an ever thinning social system being pushed to its brink by an ageing population that we need to support, but no longer feel supported by.

We're at a crossroads. We can stick to the old system and experience diminishing returns from it while we wait for technology to pick off the most repeatable, standardisable parts of our jobs (if we are lucky enough to still have jobs). We can hope that some unforeseen innovation creates masses of new full-time jobs to replace those we've already lost to larger generations above us, staying in work longer and retiring later. We can complain about how we're a smaller generation and no one listens to us or votes with us. We can sit at home, sending out CVs and covering letters— because that's what people who already have jobs tell us to do— and hope for the best. Maybe someone will give us a chance, after all.

Or…

We can use the same technologies being used against us—but for our own benefit. If businesses and governments are going to break the rules, so can we. Springing up every day are myriad new opportunities for us, if we're only willing to be both flexible and brave, to chart our own course back to prosperity. While the world is becoming increasingly difficult for people who want to be told what to do and watched while they do it, for those willing to break away from convention, it's practically an orgy of opportunity. If we so choose, we can jump long before anyone comes along to push us.

It's not that the digital age offers *less* opportunities—it just offers *very different* opportunities. The rest of this book is devoted to explaining what they are, and how you can best utilise them to create a more future-proofed life filled with greater adventure and freedom, all the while overcoming the challenges we face as a small, young generation. The freedom to:

1. Be more independent.

If the party we're born into has peaked, we can go start our own. If we feel we can't rely on our governments or employers to look after our long-term interests, the logical solution is to make ourselves less reliant on them. Luckily, that is easier than ever. As is travel. And working remotely. If we so choose, we can even create a location-free income stream that allows us to work from wherever we want, freeing us up to earn in a strong currency and live in a cheap one, and to travel as much or as little as we choose.

2. Live a life of greater travel and adventure.

While we can't control the specific opportunities that come to us in this chaotic, unfair world, we can control the number by increasing the amount of people that know about our talents. The Internet allows us to market ourselves, broadcasting our competencies and finding interesting work opportunities, and accumulating diverse life experiences unhindered by the problems of geography and seniority.

3. Try self-employment.

In the digital age, rapid change and uncertainty mean it's increasingly risky to outsource all of our economic responsibility to just one company. Self-employment was the norm at many points in human history and, slowly, for many of us, the lever is turning back to it once again. While it's not easy, and will involve many sacrifices, we'll learn how to spread our finances to minimise risk, swapping one fixed income for a variable range of incomes that complement each other; selling passively so we earn no matter where we are.

4. Create jobs that excite us.

If we don't have a boss telling us what to do, we can work on exactly what we want. We can offer the world products and services that are uniquely us, and that it's a pleasure to create and support. We can create a world where we work not because we must do so to secure our existence, but because it's the most fun way we can think of to fill our day. If we're the boss, it won't feel like work. In the beginning, we can even do this alongside our normal day jobs. It has never been easier, required less financial investment, or been less risky to try an online project. The major returns and lifestyle freedom come from replacing traditional per hour employment with owning your own business, where the value and the income produced is free to scale indefinitely.

5. Work less and live more.

Later in the book you'll hear my story, and meet many others who have created their own small Internet businesses or negotiated flexible working with their employers to make themselves location-free. If we're smart at how we finance and structure our lives, we can build one where we have to work less. We can't control the future, but we can control our reaction to it. We can increase the odds of getting what we want; the odds of our talents being discovered. While we can't control what's thrown at us, we can practice catching. We can adapt our stance from standing flat-footed at the crease to rocking back and forth on our heels in anticipation, with our heads held high, staring the horizon down, ready to swing at every opportunity that comes our way. If we do that, we'll already be better prepared than 99% of humanity.

Part 2 - Prepare.

If we accept that we're living in an increasingly changeable, volatile world, we need to prepare our lives for that, structuring them to be as future-proof as possible. Living in an uncertain world requires us to be very adaptable and flexible in how we think, live, and what we expect from others and ourselves. What follows are five essays—about failure, expectations, purpose, lifestyle creep, and personal finance—which are designed to help us mentally and financially prepare for this. In section three *Act*, we'll get more into the nitty gritty of what to do to our lifestyles.

We begin first with failure...

"I honestly think it is better to be a failure at something you love than to be a success at something you hate." – George Burns

"Failure is the tuition you pay for success." – Walter Brunell

Chapter 5 - Mental Preparation - Succeeding at Failure

With our lives increasingly uncertain and the societies and economies in which we live increasingly volatile, it's more important than ever that we have a healthy relationship to failure. If we're going to have to take more risks, logically, we're also going to fail more. With the path to prosperity less clearly marked, we're going to get lost more often along the way. There's no shame in that. Since failure is not going anywhere, we might as well befriend it. Until now, however, as humans, we've tended to live by a simple rule:

Succeed = *tell everyone!*
Fail = *quietly destroy all evidence…*

This causes a number of problems for us all. Firstly, we create an information vacuum. If we don't share our mistakes, no one else can learn from them. If we are not honest about our failures, or purport to be more successful than we really are, as well as an *information gap*, we're complicit in creating a *reality gap*. Where our failures should be laid bare—where there should be cautionary tales—there is just silence.

Into that gap rush the shameless—life's snake oil salesmen—who pretend to be successful to exploit the naiveté of others for money. These are the people who claim to earn $3000 an hour with some foolproof, work-from-home, Internet Ponzi scheme, and are kind enough to sell us their secret too, but only today, for the low, low price of just $24.99. We can buy it by clicking the big red flashing "BUY NOW" button at the very bottom of their never ending landing pages of fake testimonials and women in bikinis bent over car bonnets, being showered with hundred-dollar bills. The Internet is full of them. Your spam folder is likely to be full of them.

We should be able to read the stories of other people just like us, who have tried but not succeeded. This information could help create realistic expectations for our own endeavours. Instead, we find only people alleging how easy it is to achieve great success.

Exceptions Become Rules

The Internet makes it very easy for all of us to present a pixel-perfect, failure-free, shinier, happier digital version of ourselves. Drinking cocktails, having holidays, looking forward to the weekend. A social media highlights reel of our lives, preened and pruned and presented to our network, as if they were our everyday.

But we have to consider: If we only share the extraordinary, over time it starts to seem like everyone is living extraordinary lives— that the extraordinary is really ordinary, and anyone who isn't living an extraordinary life is failing somehow. If we behave in this manner, we all slowly, collectively chip away at *normal* until what's left is something twisted and malformed and utterly unrealistic for the average person to ever attain.

Social media is feeding this. It's a window into lives other than our own—lives of people who've made different choices than us. Have different sacrifices to us. Alternate timelines we could have taken. Different people we could have dated. Different cities we could have lived in. Different nights out we could have taken part in. But these are just snapshots. Artificial highlights. Humans naturally compare ourselves to our peers—it's why we have developed expressions like "keeping up with the Joneses." But now the Internet and social media are linking us to Joneses from different cities, countries, and cultures the world over. And those Joneses are most likely misrepresenting themselves.

If we're not careful, this can negatively affect us in our everyday lives. Choice is only good up to a limit. Then it just fatigues us. Makes it harder for us to commit to anything.[37] Makes it harder to enjoy what we've committed to. Every choice we make closes the door to other choices. If we choose to live in one city, or start a relationship with one person, we can't simultaneously also live in or date another. But social media can continuously present us with snapshots of those alternate choices and timelines. Which means, if we're not careful, we can end up sitting in a bar, with our friends, talking to our partner, living the life we've chosen, but with one eye over their shoulder, or down at our smartphones, comparing the moment we're in against those that we haven't picked and aren't experiencing. There's even a term for this now—Fear of Missing Out (FOMO)—something suggested to affect up to 70% of adults in the developed world.

A Failure to Understand the Intricacies of Success

Author David McRaney, in his book *You Are Not So Smart*, talks about how, when we sit in a crowded bar or a full restaurant, or read about the latest Internet startup to receive a multi-million-euro valuation, or the successful Facebook friend of a friend who wrote that hit novel, we forget about the empty bars and restaurants that have closed down, all the startups that went bust, all the people who tried to write a novel but dropped out by page 20. This phenomenon is called "survivorship bias." "We develop a completely inaccurate assessment of reality thanks to a prejudice that grants the tiny number of survivors the privilege of representing the much larger group to which they originally belonged.[38]" The losers, like the 90% of people whose restaurants close in the first year, disappear from view, leaving us just winners. Which makes us assume winning can't be that hard.

Researchers have also proved the existence of something called "illusory superiority," also known as the "better-than-average effect." It turns out that when we're delusional, we're usually self-servingly so, inflating our positive traits and talents and suppressing the things we're bad at. Because of the illusory superiority effect, 93% of surveyed US car drivers ranked themselves in the top 50% of drivers.[39] Likewise, 68% of teachers surveyed at one university rated themselves in the best 25% for teaching ability.[40] Prisoners rated themselves above average with respect to honesty, morality, and self-control when compared with non-prisoners, and average for law abidingness.[41] We're more likely to believe we'll own our own home, live into our 80s, and have children who are more gifted than those of our peers, and less likely to have an automobile crash, be a victim of crime, or become seriously ill.[42] Students rate themselves higher than average on positive traits, and lower than average on negative ones.[43]

As a result, we have a natural tendency to think very highly of ourselves, higher often than our own meager talents deserve. This is why, when asked to reflect honestly on our successes, we might tend to exaggerate the roles we played in achieving them, in a rush to blow our own tuneful trumpets. *It wasn't luck. It wasn't nepotism. It was talent. It was hard work. It was destiny. We were simply better than the competition.*

The Fine Line Between Success and Failure

In reality, the line between success and failure is so narrow as to be almost indistinguishable from one another. We needn't get too hung up on either. Many spectacular successes began their life as failures or accidents. Viagra was designed to treat angina. The elderly men in its control group reported it having no effect on their angina but a noticeable boost to other areas of the body. From this failure, its creator, Pfizer, stumbled upon a drug worth billions per year. The microwave oven was invented after an engineer noticed a candy bar in his pocket was being cooked by the magnetron radar device he was working on. Keith Kellogg, creator of the Kellogg's cereal company, discovered corn flakes while making bread and absentmindedly leaving boiled wheat out for a few hours, which, to his surprise, flaked when rolled. Play-doh was originally a wallpaper cleaner. Coffee was allegedly discovered after a goat herder noticed his goats became hyper after eating a certain type of berry. Potato chips were allegedly invented in an argument between a chef and a customer, in which the customer sent his potatoes back and ask for them to be sliced thinner. The chef, wanting to annoy the customer, sliced them as fine as he possibly could.

Abraham Lincoln lost his first election. Bob Dylan's high school band lost a talent contest to a tap dancing troupe. The Ford Motor Company was Henry Ford's third attempt at creating a company. "The only real mistake is the one from which we learn nothing," he would go on to say. Thomas Edison only attended school for three months and left after his teachers told him he was "too stupid to learn anything." Basketball legend Michael Jordan was cut from his high school basketball team. "When you see someone who's very successful, you almost imagine that it was a foregone conclusion, that they're a genius, that they were destined for great things,[44]" says Seth Fiegerman, creator of the website Openinglines.org, a site that interviews prominent people about setbacks in their early careers to try and dispel the myth of the overnight success. Seth started the site after being let go from his job in journalism. "I think the big takeaway is failure and setbacks, far from being uncommon, are in many ways essential."

Life is more art than science. It's more guesswork than knowledge, more blind optimism than astute rationalism. There is no blueprint. It's a mixture of hard work, adaptability, and encouraging serendipity, more commonly known as being in the right place at the right time. It's a lot about luck. Luck is to life what foreplay is to sex—while not strictly mandatory, it sure makes the ride smoother.

Along the way, failure is inevitable—maybe a little embarrassing, but not fatal. It's continuing to show up that counts. "90% of the job," as Woody Allen famously quipped.

In an uncertain world of rapid technological change, we're going to experience many ups and downs over our working lives. Skills that we've worked hard to learn will become obsolete. We will be regularly forced to reinvent ourselves, update our skills, move cities, countries, or continents to find work or better economic conditions. Our homes will rise and fall in value, making us both paper rich and paper poor, as will our savings, fluctuating our incomes and our retirement funds. Previous generations suffered similar fates, enduring wars, negative equities, hyperinflations, stock and house price crashes, as well as the usual cyclical economic booms and busts. However, if the central thesis of this book is proved correct, we're going to experience all this a lot more often.

Therefore, how we perceive each of these setbacks is going to greatly influence how much we're able to enjoy our lives. Very often, the gap between success and failure is simply so miniscule as to be indistinguishable. The factors that decide on which side we'll fall are often not in our control. So we need not revel in our glorious successes, nor lament in our embarrassing failures. What's important is just that we keep trying. Keeping being brave. Keep taking chances. Keep moving forward. Don't let our previous mistakes and so-called failures hold us back.

A farmer had only one horse. One day, his horse ran away. All the neighbors came by saying, "I'm so sorry. This is such bad news. You must be so upset?"

The man just said, "We'll see."

A few days later, his horse came back with 20 wild horses following. The man and his son corralled all 21 horses.

All the neighbors came by saying, "Congratulations! This is such good news. You must be so happy?"

The man just said, "We'll see."

One of the wild horses kicked the man's only son, breaking both his legs.

All the neighbors came by saying, "I'm so sorry. This is such bad news. You must be so upset?"

The man just said, "We'll see."

The country went to war, and every able-bodied young man was drafted to fight. The war was terrible and killed every young man, but the farmer's son was spared, since his broken legs prevented him from being drafted.

All the neighbors came by saying, "Congratulations! This is such good news. You must be so happy?"

The man just said, "We'll see.[45]"

Chapter 6 - Mental Preparation - Happiness = Reality - Expectations

In 2012, I rented an office for myself and the products of my small ecommerce business. In the larger room next door to it was a co-working space for about 10 people. During that year I started work on my first book—*How to Be German*—and occasionally in the hallway I'd meet people from the room next door and they'd tell me there was another writer in that room, called Philipp, and that he was also working on his debut novel. At the time, I knew no published authors and very little about how the publishing industry worked, and so had no real idea what "normal" was. My expectations for my book were extremely low. It seemed pretty much impossible to me that I might make a living wage from writing books. My publisher (C.H.Beck, also the publisher of this book) encouraged me to be cautiously optimistic. If we sold 10,000 copies, that would be a great success, considered a bestseller by German standards. Everyone would make money, and I'd of course be rewarded with another book deal. So, 10,000 became my benchmark for success.

I completely forgot about Philipp, the elusive writer next door. Eventually my book came out and I got busy marketing and promoting it, as it climbed towards my 10,000-book goal. After a few months and some clever online marketing it entered the Spiegel bestseller's list and reached that 10k milestone. My publisher was delighted. I was delighted. *I was a bestselling author.*

Shortly afterwards, I bumped into a girl from the room next door and she told me that Philipp, my neighbour, had published his book six months before mine. It was also a bestseller—in fact, it had been number one or two on the bestseller list for all of that time and had sold 100,000 copies!

At that moment I went from knowing no other authors to knowing one. Not some distant, famous author with which I shared nothing in common—Phillip was my age, he lived here in Berlin, and had sat on the other side of a wall from me for the previous year.

Today, my book has sold over 100,000 copies. Philipp's? *400,000 copies...*

My book's achievement is really great. But, at the back of my mind, always niggling away at me, are Philipp's sales. Something as simple as the people we know can change our opinions of our own achievements, making us feel like failures in comparison by unreasonably distorting our expectations. If I'd never met Philip, I'd probably see the sales of my book as +80,000 on my 10,000-sales target. Instead, I see it as -300,000 on his achievement, and my inherited, utterly unrealistic target.

Having met Philipp has negatively affected my overall happiness, because its raised my expectations to unrealistic levels. Where I should be comparing myself with the other 99% of writers who are unable to make a full-time living from their writing and deciding (I'm not doing all that bad at all), instead, I've managed to find an even greater outlier and taken him as my rule. This is human nature, I know—but still, it's a pretty annoying facet of it.

We already discussed in the previous chapter how important it is for us to de-criminalise and de-stigmatise failure. Expectations management goes hand in hand with that. Logically, the higher your expectations are for your life, the loftier your personal goals will be, the more vivid your imagination of what's possible, the greater height from which you're allowing yourself to fall if they are not reached. The less we expect, the lower our benchmark for success, the less we can fail, the less failure we have to mentally reconcile into some kind of positive.

Fortunately, the link between expectations and happiness turns out to be surprisingly simple—the more a situation exceeds our expectations, the happier we are. There's even a formula for it:

Happiness = reality minus expectations.

Therefore, once we know this formula, we have two options to maximise our happiness:

1. Improve reality.

This is the route most people tend to take. To work towards a better job, more money, a bigger house, a faster car, more fame and recognition. *More, more, more.* It can work, at least for a while. Like slaves to our own dopamine, we stay on the hedonistic treadmill and try and run faster and faster, outrunning our expectations.

The problem is how quickly we get use to that new, better reality. That new shiny *something*. The new smartphone, the bigger apartment, the exotic holiday, the new job title, the designer sunglasses. We're forever creating a new baseline that includes that new thing, and so we end up right back where we started again, only with higher expectations for the next thing. Every success we have raises the benchmark against which we will measure all future achievement.

In short, satisfaction is like milk—it has a very short shelf life. The alternative, however, is:

2. Lower our expectations of reality.

Rather than trying to acquire and experience more, we can focus enjoying what we already have. Instead of adding yet another thing to our to-do or bucket list, we can choose to focus instead on our already-done list. David Heinemyer Hansen, creator of successful programming languages Ruby on Rails, summarises why this is important. "When ambition is cranked up to the max due to prior accomplishments and success, it can easily provide pressure and anxiety. When that's the case, winning isn't even nearly as sweet as the loss is bitter. When you expect to win, it's merely a checked box if you do—after the initial rush of glory dies down...It goes for all walks of life. I've met many extremely accomplished people who've had the grave misfortune of reaching one too many of their goals, only to be saddled with an impossibly high baseline for success. Its devoured their intrinsic motivation, leaving nothing but an increasingly impossible search for another fix of blow-it-out-the-park success. When that doesn't happen, the withdrawal is a bitch.[46]"

Tim Urban, author of popular blog *Wait But Why,* believes that this is a particular problem for our generation. His blog post entitled "Why Generation Y Yuppies Are Unhappy" became a smash success, quickly shared, commented, and read by millions of people. It tells the story of Lucy, a disillusioned millennial. Lucy's parents (like many of ours) are Baby Boomers, born in the 1950s and raised by parents who experienced the Great Depression and fought in World War Two. Having lived a relatively modest existence, perforated by two harrowing world wars, our grandparents taught our parents' generation to have modest ambitions. Study. Work hard. Raise a family.

"They were taught that there was nothing stopping them...but that they'd need to put in years of hard work to make it happen. As the '70s, '80s, and '90s rolled along, the world entered a time of unprecedented economic prosperity. Lucy's parents, our parents, did even better than they expected to. This left them feeling gratified and optimistic." They then passed that optimism onto us. "With a smoother, more positive life experience than that of their own parents, Lucy's parents raised Lucy with a sense of optimism and unbounded possibility.[47]"

We could do anything. We were special. Our parents told us so. The media told us so. Advertising told us so. Reality TV shows full of people like us told us so. However, this enlarged our expectations for our lives and "we want to be fulfilled by our career in a way their our parents didn't think about as much," says Tim. Therefore, many of us are forced to carry the burden of an inflated sense of self that is not really in line with our actual skills and abilities. The gap between what we can offer and what we expect in return is larger and harder to jump than that of previous generations. And this is all before we take into account the negative effect that rapid technological change is doing to the number and kind of jobs available to us.

In short, we're not living in the sort of time period where we want to be saddling ourselves with too high expectations—not while so many of us are actually worse off than our parents were at the same age. It's possibly more important than ever, in fact, that we reign our expectations in to more modest levels, if we want to be happy and fulfilled in our lives. It might sound counter-intuitive at first, but I think lowering expectations is the way to a more achievable, lasting happiness. It's also surprisingly easy to do, perhaps precisely because we do it so rarely, and so we're not as hardened to the sort of psychological tricks that make it work. Here are some other techniques we could try:

1. Practice negative projection.

Stoicism has an idea called *negative projection*. It's like a form of rather morbid meditation. The idea is that you should take a few minutes out of your everyday to quietly imagine everything that you hold dear being taken from you. All of it. Your loved ones, your career, your wealth, your health. Everything that you couldn't imagine losing, you should imagine losing.

Sounds fun, right?

There is a certain logic behind negative projection that makes it very valuable. Merely by thinking the unthinkable, you make it possible. You're not allowing yourself to take what you have for granted, and you can start, mentally at least, to explore the consequences of your actions and what you might do should your own personal life Hiroshima occur.

I practice negative projection from time to time and I find it just the right sort of jarring. It reminds me how much I have in my life that I would be afraid to lose. For example, I find, on days when I've spent just 10 minutes negative projecting my imminent demise, I react differently to the sound of my girlfriend coming back home from work. Normally, I'm too busy with whatever I'm doing to really notice. Or I'll notice, and resent her intrusion into my work. Or, I'll remember that she wanted me to do something, like the hoovering or emptying the bins, and that, as per usual, I haven't done it. I'll hope we don't argue about that and lose the better part of our evening.

However, on negative projection days, I'll usually find myself stopping work and perhaps even smiling at the sound of her key entering the front door's lock. Because it's on these days that I fully appreciate that she had a choice that evening, as she has every evening, and that she picked to come home to me.

Probably you've had a brief taste of the power of negative projection in your own life when you've woken up following a nightmare in which your partner has cheated on you, or you've fallen off a cliff, or your pet dog is run over by an ice cream truck, or your child gets sick. Whatever the scenario, however implausible, you feel great relief when you wake up and your partner is still lying there next to you, the dog is curled up in his bed, your child is healthy, and the world is normal again. That normal suddenly feels extra special because you better appreciate its fragility.

2. Take lean months.

I first read about this idea in the hit book *The Four-Hour Work Week* by US-American author Tim Ferris. Every few months, Tim artificially reduces his standard of living. If he would usually stay in a four-star hotel, he downgrades to a two-star. If he would normally spend €100 a week on groceries, as a challenge, he'll limit himself to €15. It's like giving up some of life's luxuries for Lent, so we take them less for granted. We could try reducing your grocery bills for a week, unplugging our satellite televisions for a month, not use the car for a fortnight, or try to live on the financial equivalent of Hartz Vier for a month. Just as with stoicism's negative projection, we're giving ourselves a little taste of what we fear, in the hope that:

A) We remind ourselves how lucky we are to have our comparably luxurious lifestyle.

B) We remember how adaptable we are.

Friends that do the same thing report a similar outcome. The new becomes the normal remarkably quickly. After a few days you stop craving chocolate. You get used to travelling with the bus, and actually appreciate having time to read a book or listen to music. You rediscover how good those cheap biscuits you used to eat as a student but didn't buy for years still taste. You take that negative and find some kind of way, even if it's totally irrational, to make a positive out of it.

You realise how that thing that you had in your life that you couldn't imagine giving up is actually just another luxury, not a necessity. In doing so, you help create a new, more realistic, affordable normal, and become less scared at the idea of potentially having to scale back your lifestyle at some point in the future, which is an inevitability if you follow the advice in later parts of this book.

3. Challenge our sense of entitlement.

A friend told me a story about one of her colleagues, Lisa. In my friend's company, there are no set car parking spaces. There are enough spaces for everyone, and in theory anyone can park anywhere, although over time people have naturally started to develop habits about which spaces they like to park in. Lisa has taken this to an extreme. The way my friend tells it, she already knows just by the look on Lisa's face when she walks in to the office whether or not someone has parked in Lisa's regular parking space. Because Lisa has decided that she owns the space that she regularly parks in, and so feels justified in throwing a hissy fit if anyone dares to park in "her space," because "everyone knows that is my space!"

By deciding that she owns it and is in fact entitled to park there, she allows herself to get annoyed when someone takes from her what was is not hers in the first place, and that she has no actual, legitimate rights to. This sense of entitlement, even over a minor thing like a parking space, is an example of how our outlook can negatively affect our happiness, if we let it—whether in our families, in our jobs, or our careers. The higher our expectations, the greater our sense of our entitlement and the greater the discomfort when those things are taken from us.

In conclusion, if we strive for perfection, we can only ever fail. Lasting happiness comes not from allowing our imaginations to run wild, darting around the present with its red pen, critiquing everything and marking areas for improvement. Lasting happiness is found in practicing being present and appreciative of all that we already have and how much we'd hate to lose it—to forget any naive belief we may have in some idealised happy ever after, or sentimental misremembering of the past, in favour of embracing the messy, imperfect reality that is our present.

In the beginning, God created the earth, and he looked upon it in his cosmic loneliness.

And God said, "Let Us make living creatures out of mud, so the mud can see what We have done." And God created every living creature that now moveth, and one was man. Mud as man alone could speak. God leaned close to mud as man sat, looked around, and spoke. "What is the purpose of all this?" he asked politely.

"Everything must have a purpose?" asked God.

"Certainly," said man.

"Then I leave it to you to think of one for all this," said God.

And He went away.
— Kurt Vonnegut, Cat's Cradle

Chapter 7 - Mental Preparation - We Will Never Know What We Want

See if this sounds familiar—you notice something that you want to fix in your life, whether it's getting to work earlier, losing weight, being more productive after lunch, or not swearing at your children when they refuse to go to sleep. You decide to tackle this problem head on, and either devise or research an AMAZING LIFE HACK to help you. It might be the daily seven-minute power workout; the *no-snooze morning*; the *only eat pineapples* fad diet; the *count to ten, Zen* parenting plan. The exact specifics of the AMAZING LIFE HACK are not really important. You incorporate AMAZING LIFE HACK into your day-to-day life. The people around you are skeptical about it. But you're confident. Day one is a little bit difficult as you adjust, but by day two and three you're already hitting your stride.

You love AMAZING LIFE HACK!

It's such a positive change. You feel great. You're not sure why you've only just discovered AMAZING LIFE HACK now, after all these wasted years. You start to evangelise AMAZING LIFE HACK to your friends and family. You share it with your online friends and followers—"The secret to weight loss = pineapples! IT REALLY WORKS! Try it! http://fadpineapplediet.com."

Then, slowly, your commitment to AMAZING LIFE HACK starts to wane. It gets a bit hard. Or a bit boring. Or too pineappl*ey*. You make your first excuse to not do AMAZING LIFE HACK. It's fine to take a day off, you tell yourself—you'll be twice as dedicated to AMAZING LIFE HACK the next day, which will more than compensate.

Only, then, the next day, you don't do it either. Nor the day after that. Slowly, AMAZING LIFE HACK, this thing that was really working and totally life-changing, is no longer working, and then, finally, is simply no longer a thing. At least not in your life. You forget about it. Your friends forget about it.

Normality resumes. Time passes. You can no longer even look at a pineapple anymore.

Then, a while later, you notice something else that you don't like in your life—maybe you're not spending enough time with friends, you're losing control of your inbox, you're spending too long on Facebook, or you've developed a fear of pineapples—and you decide to do something about that. In fact, you've read about this great idea to solve it...it's called AMAZING LIFE HACK 2.

The whole cycle repeats. Forever. This is your life.

Why is this? Why, despite the best of our intentions, can't we commit to things we know will improve our lives? Why do we seem to want one thing one minute, and something completely different the next? Why do we react to a looming deadline by ignoring it until the last possible moment? Why are we so damn irrational?

In the 1920s, the Chicago Electric Company undertook a famous study on human productivity. Their management, like all good management, wanted to find new ways of raising the productivity of staff. So they commissioned researchers to undertake a test within one of their factories, called the Hawthorne Works factory. Researchers would alter certain variables like heating or lighting, and would record if it made the production lines more or less productive. The staff were informed that the test was taking place.

The results didn't quite go to plan, but revealed something important about the human condition. The first test was to increase the brightness of the lights in the factory. This raised productivity—which probably seemed logical, as the better people could see, the faster they could work, right? *Brighter lights = higher productivity.* But just to be sure, they decided to lower the lights to below the normal levels. While they might have expected productivity to decrease to below normal levels, surprisingly, they found that productivity increased *yet again*. Higher still than with the brighter lighting.

Higher or lower lights = higher productivity? Strange.

Then they changed the heating, and found that, yet again, as long as they changed it, whether they made it hotter or colder, with each new test, productivity increased.

From this, they concluded that it was not *what* they were changing, but *the fact that they were changing things* that lead to the increase in productivity. It was the extra focus placed on the workers that was making them extra productive in response. This was later coined The Hawthorne Effect.

Something similar is happening with AMAZING LIFE HACK. It's our own Hawthorne Effect. We lose weight (at first) not because of the specifics of our new miracle fad pineapple diet, but because we start paying attention to what we eat (where before, we ate anything that was foolish enough to come within reach of our arms). We get up earlier (at first) not because of our no-snooze program, but because we have decided to do something about our laziness. We stop swearing at our children (at first) not because counting to 10 reduces our desire to hurl the F-work at them, but because we've decided that swearing at our children is bad enough to warrant special attention to fix it.

Only, over time, we're unable to sustain that focus on the problem and maintain the special effort to fix it, and so we slip back to our old selves.

Like most people with too much time on my hands, I enjoy making myself miserable by reading self-help books. I think most self-help books tend to disappoint because they forget all this. They exaggerate a) how rational we are and b) that we're somehow the best judges of what we want. They tend to focus too much on the *what*—the variable that we should change—just like the light or the heating in Chicago Electric Company's factory. But it's not the *what* that matters. It's not the specifics of AMAZING LIFE HACK that are important. Exercising choice and control over our circumstances feels good, regardless of the specific choice or method of control we choose. We're putting ourselves in charge. We're not letting ourselves be victims of our circumstances. The freedom to choose is in many ways just as or even more important than the actual choice we make—more than the specific brightness or heat setting we pick for the production line of our lives.

Humans = Irrationality

Another shortcut to disappointment comes from overestimating our own rationality. I've read many self-help books that do this. They see us as inputs, processes, and outputs—like a car. Petrol goes in, forward motion and exhaust fumes come out. If you put the same amount of petrol in tomorrow, the same amount of forward motion and exhaust fumes will come out. Therefore, the job of the self-help book is to help us identify and fix whatever flaw in our design—whatever errant process in our being—is causing our engines to backfire, or that annoying warning light on the dashboard of our lives to blink.

However, there's a lot of research to suggest that we're just not very rational. For example, did you know that bronze medal winners actually report higher happiness than that of silver medal winners, even though they've finished in a lower position?[48] Or that people feel more certain that they will win a lottery if they can control the numbers on their tickets? Or that they are more confident that they will win a dice toss if they can throw the dice themselves?[49] In some situations, it is actually manic depressives, not normally functioning people, that can more rationally analyse their lives. And surprisingly, poor people who are getting richer are happier than rich people getting poor, even if the rich people are many times richer than the poor people?[50] Similarly, when researchers asked people if they'd prefer to have a job in which they earn $30,000 the first year, $40,000 the next, and $50,000 in year three, or a job that paid $60,000 in year one, $50,000 in year two, and finally $40,000 in year three, people usually picked the first option even though they'd be $10,000 better off if they picked the second.[51] For further examples, I again recommend Daniel Gilbert's *Stumbling on Happiness*, the wisest, funniest book on the absurdities of being human that I've had the pleasure to read.

In psychology circles, this phenomenon is called dysrationalia, and is defined as "the inability to think and behave rationally despite adequate intelligence.[52]" This explains why otherwise smart people might still believe in horoscopes or aliens, bet on black after several reds in roulette (believing black must be due), or fall victims to cults or religions despite no evidence for these beliefs.

Rather than working like a car, we're more like a magician's top hat. There are inputs—a playing card, someone's watch, a wallet, a magic wand—but out might come a fluffy white rabbit. The watch might morph into a never-ending chain of brightly coloured handkerchiefs. Maybe the wallet disappears entirely. What happens in the middle? Who knows? It's a mystery. A black box. Some call it magic. You could probably also call it *being human.*

Ironically, often the thing that stops us acknowledging this irrationality *is* the irrationality. This is similar to us thinking we're smarter than we are. Or better drivers. We think we're more rational. Other people might be tricked by their cognitive biases, but we're fine. As a result, we're often too irrational to recognise when we're behaving irrationally—and even if we do, too irrational to then fix it. It's like asking a bank robber to catch himself. It's a curious form of something called the Dunning-Kruger Effect, in which people are too stupid to know they are stupid, which is why they are just as confident in their decisions as smart people (usually more so, in fact). It's nice to think we're in control of our lives and can predict our behavior—that how we think, feel, and behave today is likely to predict how we will tomorrow; that past performance *is* an indicator of future success; that if we get married, we'll stay faithful to our spouse; that if an old lady needs help crossing the road, we'll help; that if that same old lady needs help tomorrow but it is raining or we're late to pick up the kids from school, we'll still help. Because we're nice, helpful people. Reliable. Civic minded.

In reality, we're a portable mixed bag of personalities, experiences, expectations, and neuroses. Always in flux. While one part of us wants to help that old lady, the other part just wants her to get out of the way so that we can get back to solving whatever small problem it is that is stressing us out. Meanwhile, another deeply repressed part of our brains just wants to run her down in our car, for sport. Our brains and bodies are a combination of different subsystems, with different wants and needs often directly at odds with each other. While one part might wants us to rest, the other wants us to be productive; one is longing for solitude to process new experiences, while the other wants the stimulus of company to create new ones. Josh Kaufmann talks about this conflict in his book *The Personal MBA*[53]: "The situation is akin to a heater and an air conditioner fighting to control the temperature in a single room. As long as their respective reference levels are mutually exclusive, neither will ever be under control—they'll continue to expend effort to move the system in the direction they're controlling for."

There is always this inner conflict, and something as simple as how hungry we are, our blood sugar levels, how much willpower we've already exerted on other temptations, or just the time of day can influence which of those subsystems wins and gets control.

We'll never know what we want, because we want everything and also nothing.

If we forget this, however, it's easy to get frustrated by our inability to behave as people expect us to, and, in turn, how we expect ourselves to. We know that we sit in the driving seats of our lives. But we don't understand why the vehicle that we're driving doesn't respond as we would like it to. Why yesterday it went fast when we had nothing important to do, yet today, when we've somewhere to be or some deadline to meet, we can't get moving at all. No matter how much we sit there and kick our legs in frustration, it makes no difference—in fact, often the angrier we get, the more we complain, the more certain we are about who we are and what we want, and the more the different parts of us try and sabotage us.

We don't need to cure this irrationality. It's central to who we are, and it would be futile to even try—like shouting at a lemon for not being an orange. You can do it, but it won't get you anywhere, and you'll still be left with a lemon afterwards. *We are lemons.* We need to try and use that to our lemony advantage, and get good at making martinis. Rather than trying to fight our inner irrationality, we can, instead, accept that:

- We'll never know what we want.

- If we had what we wanted, we wouldn't want it anymore.

- Most of the time we just want the freedom to want the opposite of what we have—but not to act upon this want.

- The choice is usually as important as what we actually choose.

I've developed some techniques to incorporate all these ideas into my own life. Maybe they will also help you.

1. If it works, it works—regardless of why it works.

I'm always trying to find new ways to write more words each day. I've tried so many different AMAZING LIFE HACKS—writing in the morning, writing late at night, a Zen writing program with no functions (not even save), having a word goal each day, writing from my office, writing from home, writing from cafes, writing standing up. Each time, I usually get that initial high and boost of productivity, then it quickly drops off again. However, if all it takes to be temporarily more productive is to change a variable, a *what*—the time I work, from where I work, what software I use—I can keep changing variables. It doesn't matter how irrational it is. It doesn't matter that I know it is irrational. Just that it works. I can change a new variable every week if that's what little irrational me needs. A new office, a new chair, a new morning routine, a new exercise routine, a new approach to writing, a new note-taking trick. New cafe. New coffee. New office. New restaurant. Write on the train. Write in the park. Write while standing on my head. Whatever. The *what* is not important. It doesn't have to make sense. I don't have to make sense. I just have to work with my irrationality, not against it.

If I like changing things, I should structure my life in such a way that I have the freedom to keep changing things.

2. Stop seeing yourself as one person.

Recently I spotted some unwelcome growth around my midriff, a classic symptom of too much chocolate and not enough exercise. I decided to do something about it. I thought back to how much fun playing football was in my youth, where I used to play every night after school. I thought about the trance-like state you can enter where the tiny, petty problems of the everyday yield to the heightened concentration and muscle memory of sport.

I found a nice group of people that play football together every Tuesday and Friday in a nearby park. The first Tuesday that I played I had great fun. My quest was over. I'd found my group, and I came home and happily made a reoccurring Google calendar event for every Tuesday and Friday: *Football in the park*.

On Friday morning I got the first *Football in the park* email reminder: "Oh, good, football again," I said to myself. I played, and it was nice. The next Tuesday I got another reminder: *Football in the park*. "Ah, football. Hmm. Okay," I said. I played, and it was nice. I'm guessing you can see how the pattern is developing here. The third time I got that reminder, I didn't really want to play anymore. I began to resent the commitment me of the past had made as I imagined hypothetical football playing. *The goals I would score, the friends I would make, the weight I would lose* met the imperfect reality of *the goals I wouldn't score, the odd person who would annoy me, the effort of biking there, the injuries, rain, etc.*

I also no longer felt I was choosing to play football, but rather having it expected of me by an earlier version of myself. I like playing football. However, it turns out I only want to play when I want to play, and I want to decide that on a whim, about 15 minutes beforehand. Otherwise, the *me of the past* is making a commitment that the *me of today* has to keep, and it resents him for it.

As a result of this, I've taken to thinking of myself as three separate people: *Past*, *Present* and *Future*, like Scrooge's ghosts. As is so often the case with family, the three of *me* know they are related, but that doesn't mean that they have to like each other.

Past Me is the hardest to fathom, but easiest to fix. He's happy when *Present Me* and *Future Me* are getting on. Then we create the kind of happy memories that make him comfortable back there in the past. Otherwise he second-guesses and undermines *Present Me* with the indiscretions, mistakes, and missed opportunities of my yesteryears. I try hard not to listen to him, but I know I'll spend much more time with him when I get older and my quality of life and time horizons change, removing some of *Present Me* and *Future Me's* sheen.

Present Me is an out and out hedonist—the first guy on life's dance floor. He has a perception of time that stretches to about an hour in the future and an hour in the past. He lives in the moment, chasing the next quick high. This is because the consequences of his actions are not *his* problem—that's for *Future Me* and *Past Me* to deal with. If he jumps me off a bridge, it's *Future Me* that gets lumbered with the broken ankle and *Past Me* that has to justify his decision-making or learn to live with its regrets.

Future Me is the most complicated. He's like the problem aunt that you dread getting a visit from, because you know she is going to look down her nose at how you live, and tell you that you should have a better job, a cleaner bathroom, and that you've not saved enough towards your pension.

Of course, the three me's are an oversimplification, and not this distinct. They all exist and influence each other all the time, in real time. But dividing them in this way helps me understand myself better—helps me understand why what worked yesterday and made me happy then makes me slightly less happy today, and will probably make me slightly less happy tomorrow. Because yesterday that project I was so excited about when it was just an idea has become actual work that I'm dumping on to *Future Me*. But not only that, now it is a real thing I've committed to. If I quit it, *Past Me* will have to live with that failure, or try and rationalise something positive out of it. It also explains to me why I often don't even want to do really fun things like playing football, if those really fun things have been scheduled in advance. *Future Me* and *Present Me* want flexibility. They want the freedom to indulge in their irrationality. Or irresponsibility. They want the freedom to choose more than they actually care what they will pick. They want to make their own decisions—especially if those decisions will be to do the exact opposite of what the other *me*'s, and all of my many sub-systems, rationally want them to pick.

3. Limit the length of commitments.

Building on this idea, a friend of mine is a project manager, and told me about a rule for IT projects: For any IT project that last longer than one year, with every month that passes, the odds the project will be completed successfully and in-budget drop by around 5%. This is because the needs of the company when the project started, more than one year back, are likely to have changed. So, the longer the project rolls on, the more likely it is that this awesome new system is solving a problem that simply no longer exists. The company and its processes have changed too much in that year. As far as IT projects are concerned, shorter is better. This is often summarised down to "release early, release often," which is also fine advice medical advice if you get it from your doctor. I think the same logic that applies to IT projects applies to us. Commitments— whether they be in our careers, finances, or emotions—increase in risk the longer we must remain committed to them. So I try not to.

As a result, things like marriage are not an option for me. I simply can't forecast my desires that far in advance, and don't want to place that kind of emotional constraint on myself. Or course, other people get married. Or buy houses. Or adopt dogs. Or have children. Or begin careers in dentistry. All long bets. That doesn't mean they're idiots or that they'll fail, or even that they don't really know themselves. It just means that they're more comfortable making bigger bets and believe they know better what they'll want on Wednesday 13th March 2024 than I dare to ask of myself. Of course, as I get older, it's possible my time horizons will broaden, or that the three me's will feel more in sync. I'd be fine with that.

And of course, even those commitments that appear to be long-term can usually be shorted on a whim. You can always sell houses. You can divorce partners. You can leave a promising career in dentistry. But that doesn't mean you'll have the guts to do so. Think about the people you know who stay in marriages that aren't working, or in jobs that they hate because, as unhappy as they make them, they can always justify them in some clever way (such as "better the devil you know," "if it's not broken, why fix it?" or "I'm lucky to even have a job in the first place." If you don't first back yourself into a corner, you then don't have to spend time justifying to yourself how much you like that corner—and that you, yourself, picked it.

Because of my in-built irrationality, my desire for choice, long-term commitments stressing me out, and the three different me's, I've found that the easiest way for me to organise my life is to make as few demands on *Present* and *Future Me* as possible. That means no major financial commitments. No high monthly rent. No mortgage payments. Nothing that locks me into a fixed, regular, scheduled nine-to-five job or project. Nothing that would require me to live in one location, with no chance to flee if I so choose.

Fortunately, this kind of lifestyle is also perfectly in sync with a world of rapid change, as depicted in the rest of this book. While I'm mostly advocating protecting ourselves against our own whims, this approach also prepares us for economic and employment uncertainty—where we might quickly have to react to losing our jobs, our businesses losing major customers, or an unexpected rent increase. With rapid technological innovation reducing permanence in jobs, economies, relationships, and lifestyles, it's more important than ever to build a life that can flex, in just the same way that earthquake-proof buildings flex. Those buildings, like our lives, can still have strong central columns—our health, our friendships, our work—but they don't treat them as immovable. They are free to tilt and turn, and so ride out the inevitable shocks that are going to come our way.

It might seem like what I'm looking to do is minimise risk, but that's not the case. Risk is good. It's intrinsically linked in our heads to reward. If you go to the zoo, you can see animals living in a specially controlled environment, with enough food and free from the threat of predators. Do they look particularly happy to you? No. If we make our lives too safe and secure, the end result above a certain point is not that we get happier, but that, just like those animals, we end up feeling trapped. We should be free to follow up on every stupid idea we have, every fleeting something that interrupts our sleep and sends us rushing off for a notepad to record it. Every pipe dream, daydream, and ridiculous fantasy that excites us. We want more of that. It's those moments we are after—when our hearts beat faster, when our breath is less laboured, when our life is more spontaneous, when we do something that surprises ourselves, when we feel a spark of life that shoots up our backs and necks and raises the hairs of our arms in a short, sharp shock of possibility. We should be free to grab at all of those moments, if we so choose to. Or, just to enjoy the possibility of them, the belief that we could choose them, even if we never actually do. That kind of freedom comes from structuring our lives flexibly.

What I'm encouraging in this book is not minimising risk—it's minimising burden. So it's to our financial burdens that we turn next.

"Wealth consists not in having great possessions, but in having few wants." — Epictetus

Chapter 8 - Financial Preparation - Lifestyle Creep

At Microsoft, I worked with a data analyst from New Zealand called Steve. Steve was a lovable, down-to-earth Kiwi who ended up, somehow, I think more by luck than foresight, working in a high pressure corporate environment like Microsoft. Previously he'd been a marine biologist, and would boast about entire months spent masturbating salmon or doing Pavlov's Dog-style experiments on goldfish (in case you are wondering, Steve proved that they can learn to associate the sound of a bell to either pleasure or pain, depending on what follows it). What I liked most about Steve was that he didn't take anything or anyone too seriously, and you knew that one day he was going to leave the corporate world of spreadsheets and sales meetings, buy a yacht, crash it drunk into a cove, and never be heard from again.

How he ended up working with us—and why he stayed there—I'm not sure. I think he figured that at some point they'd get around to firing him (and probably me with him), and until then he was taking the perks and waiting it out. Not that he wasn't good at his job— because he was. It was just that he wasn't one of the frenzied in-at-8am-home-at-8pm-email-on-the-weekend career-minded people that Microsoft liked so much. He was just goofy, fish-loving Steve.

Much to both of our surprise, after I'd been at Microsoft for nearly a year, Steve was offered a promotion to become the data analytics team lead. It would mean he'd be responsible for a team of five data analysts. Naturally, this greater responsibility would be compensated by a pay rise of about €12k a year. Currently, he managed himself, and judging by the amount of days he'd arrived late, hung-over, or wearing his shirt inside out, he wasn't even doing that very well. But he was good at his job. He produced a lot of valuable intelligence for the sales team about which leads to target, and then spent the rest of the day sending me weird fish porn.

Steve was flattered by the offer, but torn. It was a promotion, and of course he was already imagining what he might do with that extra €1k per month (before tax, of course). He didn't really need the money—Microsoft pays well, and we lived in Reading, which is a reasonably priced (albeit very boring) city in the south of England.

He mulled it over for a night and decided to take the job. To celebrate, we went out for some beers, and the next evening he proudly showed off to me the giant new smart TV he'd just brought via the company store for €1k. You may recognise this reaction to a sudden windfall. It's the *Oh my god, I've got money, what shall I buy? This? Yes. This. I'll take four please* response.

I left the company shortly after (I wasn't even fired!), but we met up some eight months later at an Irish bar in central London. *It was like meeting a different man.*

I almost didn't recognize him as he entered the pub. He'd gained at least 10kg in weight, adding a paunch and an extra layer of skin around his neck. He looked tired and washed out. Where before he'd had a very cheeky playful sense of humour, he now rarely seemed to joke, and I noticed that he looked at his watch a lot. I asked how the new job was, and he said that, immediately after being promoted, the pressure had greatly increased. Where before he could bumble along doing what was asked of him, now he was supposed to be "proactive." To work under his own initiative. To create and supervise the work others did, while doing just as much of his own work as before. On top of that, he no longer had to answer just for himself, but for the whole team.

"Staff management. It's awful," he said, shaking his head and slowly nursing at his beer.

"Really? I thought you might like some little mini-Steves to order around?"

"Yeah, at first. For about five minutes. But then they want things. *Advice, guidance, holidays*. They have problems. Individually they're great, but together, as a team? They fight and bicker. Humans are basically just problem generation devices."

His team was only five people, but two didn't get along and were always squabbling and trying to undermine each other. Another team member had sickness issues, and yet another was immune to overtime and so considered a slacker by the rest. As a senior manager, even if he'd completed all his work, he could not be seen to leave at 6pm. That would imply he didn't have enough work to do, wasn't taking his responsibilities seriously, wasn't the career man that they wanted him to be. So he often just sat around at the office waiting for the rest of the management team to leave, so that he could to.

"Oh well, at least you got a raise out of it," I offered.

Steve sighed. "It wasn't worth it. After tax, and the extra things I've brought, I barely notice the difference."

"If you could go back to before," I asked, "would you still accept the promotion?"

He thought about it a few seconds. "No. Not knowing what I know now."

Of course, it's hard to judge Steve too harshly, because it's so easy to recognise parts of ourselves in his behaviour, and to imagine that we would have done just as he did. Of course, it's great for our egos to be wanted, to have someone say, "You are doing a great job, here is a slightly more challenging one and we'll pay you more to complete it," just as happened to Steve. He was flattered, imagined the extra money would have made him happier than it actually did, and by then had already inflated his lifestyle to match this new income.

For most of us, life develops in a similar way—we get a job, and that job pays us a certain amount. Because of this information, we make financial decisions, like which type of car we drive, how many bedrooms our house has, and how exotic of a destination we'll visit on our annual holiday. We work that job for all it's worth, then we go out to find a better one, which usually means one that offers more money and status.

Just as Steve did.

However, now that we have a higher income, we upgrade certain parts of our lives. New toys. New accessories. New homes. Like leveling up a computer game character. The kitchen in our current apartment has always annoyed us, right? It is a little dark. Plus, the dining room is too small to have those dinner parties we like to throw, isn't it? So, we upgrade to somewhere bigger.

Woohoo! Progress!

Then, however, we find that we now have new problems. Like, all this new space to fill in our bigger place. It should really be filled with nice, quality furniture befitting a person of our newly increased status, shouldn't it? Since our work hours have also increased with our heightened responsibilities, we also need time-saving devices like a dishwasher or a robotic vacuum cleaner. We even find ourselves strangely drawn to the sorts of extravagant trinkets *past us* would have mocked mercilessly as pointless or extravagant—a cleaner, heated towel rails, a set of expensive knives, good wine, a lemon hat, etc.

As a result of all this slow, continual upgrading, our monthly financial outgoings increase, adapting to the size of our new higher income. We find that, once all of this is paid for, there isn't much difference in our bank account at the end of each month. The more we earn, the more we spend. This is called lifestyle creep, or lifestyle inflation, and it's a serious problem.

Because, as obvious as it sounds, the more our employer pays us, the more they will expect from us. So as our wages increase, so do our work hours, which leaves us more stressed and with less time to spend in that larger apartment, driving that new car, watching that new €1k TV, or using our lemon hat. Even when we do have time, we can find our thoughts are more often consumed with work, the monkey on our backs.

The less free time we have, the more we want from that free time—and justifiably so. We want to be compensated for how hard we work and how much stress we have. How often do you hear people say things like "I work hard. Don't I deserve expensive shoes? Or a five-star holiday? Or a nice home to come back to? Or to eat in a fancy restaurant?" So we treat ourselves to those things.

But since we get so quickly used to any temporary boosts in lifestyle if we are not very, very careful, it is easy to simply keep lumbering ourselves with an ever higher monthly financial commitment, which means we'll always need to work that hard and earn that much to pay for it, even if in the end it leaves us no happier than our previous diet lifestyle. The problem is how quickly we get used to things, whether it's new apartments or swimming in waterfalls. This is usually referred to as the Hedonic Treadmill. If our fixed costs increase, such as our rent or mortgage payments, they can become a ball and chain that stops us doing something else. They can forcibly bind us to our current standard of living, making it difficult for us to leave our jobs, or become paranoid about losing them. This paranoia might well be valid, because of rapid technological change affecting our industry. Therefore, the single most important thing we can do, after preparing mentally, is to prepare ourselves financially for an increasingly uncertainty life. One of the biggest barriers to this is lifestyle creep.

It's not that our happiness is fixed. It does fluctuate, and we can increase it—just not as much as we usually imagine, and not because of the things we usually think. A famous study in this area compared the happiness over time of lottery winners, people paralysed in an accident, and a control group. Surprisingly, all three reported similar levels of happiness. Lottery winners, after they'd had time to adjust to their win, were no happier than paralysed people after they'd had the same time to adapt to their new disability.[54] Similar research has concluded that getting divorced, the death of a spouse, having a child, and getting married all do not alter our long-term happiness. There may be a temporary dip or increase, but over time we return to our usual base level. Our income, our physical attractiveness, and even our health are all poor indicators of our happiness levels.[55]

The best indicator? The quality of our inter-personal relationships.[56] A study published in the *Journal of Socio-Economics* found that increasing our "social involvement" could make us as happy as an extra €90k a year.[57] What do you need to cultivate great inter-personal relationships? Mostly, you need time. Something Steve no longer had.

Of course, it takes great courage to turn down a promotion and decide we are happy where we are, that we have all that we need, that we want as much time as possible to spend with our friends and family, and that anything else that we introduce into our lives is just something else we'll have to pay for or be afraid to lose. Interestingly, not only did those lottery winners not get happier after their win, they also were found to take "significantly less pleasure from a series of mundane events.[58]" Not only does lifestyle creep mean we get used to that new upgraded thing, but it also takes the sheen off of the old thing that we used to like so much, but now find inadequate in comparison.

I've thought a lot about this problem, and come up with what I hope is a simpler way of getting control of our finances and fighting against the evils of lifestyle creep. I call it *The Freedom Figure*. It's the topic of the next chapter.

"The biggest risk of all—not doing what you want today on the belief you can buy the right to do it tomorrow." – Unknown

Chapter 9 - Financial Preparation - The Freedom Figure

One of my old high school friends has a curious relationship with money that, I fear, is depressingly common. It's as if, at a very young age, someone told him bank notes are like Mission Impossible briefings. *They self-destruct.* Therefore, the best thing to do is just spend money as soon as you receive it, preferably in creative, reckless, and entertaining ways. This is what he does with his wages, without fail, every month. There is no relationship between his income and his savings, because he doesn't have any savings and there's no indication he would, no matter the size of his income. Yes, he's that creative, reckless, and entertaining...

When he was a cleaner, he earned about €10k a year, and spent about €12k a year. Then he was a self-employed courier and earned about €12k a year, and spent about €14k a year. Now he's an employed courier and earns around €21k a year, and spends about €23k a year. Not satisfied with his earnings and never having any money, he is usually juggling a variety of credit cards, loans, and terrible get-rich-quick schemes that he's discovered on the Internet, which promise great reward for minimal time and talent— whether it be from selling fake clothing, joining a betting syndicates, or reselling concert tickets.

These schemes rarely ever work, because his starting point is always *With what can I make the most money, doing the least possible work?* rather than *With what unique combination of my skills can I solve people's problems?* which is usually a better starting point for making money—but we'll get to that in later chapters.

As a result of his lack of prudence, after 12 years of employment, his net assets are €0. He's worked for 12 years to get exactly back to where he started. Since he's also acquired a variety of overdrafts and credit card debts, I think it's probably accurate to say he's worked 12 years to become worse off than when he started, but that's too depressing to think about, so let's not.

Recently, he wanted to borrow some money from me because he'd purchased a bunch of tickets for a concert he thought would sell out, but now hadn't, and he wanted to hold on to them and sell them last minute. But that left him without any cash for other bills.

I just asked him one question: *Why?*

Why, when he knows he spends everything he earns, the second he earns it, and the net result is always that he has no money, does he create stress for himself with these get-rich-quick schemes? Does he ever calculate how many hours he invests in them? How much extra stress they cause him? Like most people, if he earns €25k, he'll spend €27k; if he earns €27k, he'll spend €30k; €40k and he'll probably spend €45; and so on and so forth.

Of course, I understand his behaviour because I used to be the same as him when I lived in the UK. I would spend everything I had every month. I had various overdrafts and credit cards, and I'd juggle my money across them. No matter how much I earned, I just couldn't quite seem to get ahead of myself. Like him, my lifestyle was always a reaction to my income, which is like picking a meal based on the cost, not how hungry you are.

Now, remember, the goal of this book is not only to show how to best avoid being replaced by a robot, but also to show how you can use technology to create a life of greater freedom and adventure. The single most important step in this process is getting control of your finances. Good financial management, while not sexy, is the foundation upon which everything else is built. If we make those foundations strong, and fight lifestyle creep's attempts to weaken them, we can survive more of what life throws at us—whether it's a redundancy, a period of retraining, or a temporary health setback.

Without it, as soon as we have one setback, either it it's all reduced to rubble, or we have to go into debt, which is just a temporary fix that only makes it even more likely that the whole thing will collapse with our next major financial setback.

The Freedom Figure - Separating Lifestyle from Income

I did finally work out a system for controlling my finances. The turning point for me was becoming self-employed. Because I often had nothing coming in, I had to watch everything that went out. I had to downscale and simplify. My system worked so well for me that now, some five years of self-employment later, I finally have something called *savings*. I never thought that day would arrive. Sometimes I log into my bank account just to look at them. It feels very strange and eerily adult. In reality, I no longer need to look at my bank account at all because my Freedom Figure system works so well. My money is managing itself. But I actually enjoy looking, so I still do.

The Freedom Figure system is designed to fight against lifestyle creep. Its aim is to totally forget about income and assume that our income has no major bearing on the core decisions of our lives, such as where we live, how we live, and how we work. How much we need to earn is what we decide last and rationally (as much as is possible, being as irrational as we are), only after we've analysed and audited our lifestyles. This is the exact opposite of how most people, like my friend, or Steve, or *past me*, normally do it.

It's a deceptively simple system. In fact, it is mostly just calculating one number. Here is my Freedom Figure:

Freedom Figure Breakdown

Fixed Costs

Rent - €520 – Rent for my modest 52m² apartment, in Berlin, including all bills.

Insurances - €220 - Health insurance

Monthly Subscriptions - €27.89
- €9.95 - GEZ Bastards
- €9.95 - Spotify Subscription
- €7.99 - Netflix Subscription

Total Fixed Costs - €767.89

Variable Costs

Food/drink - €200 (for my €50 weekly shop)

Entertainment - €25 - Books (since I only read English books, the libraries in Berlin rarely have what I'm looking for, so I still buy books. I buy five per month at an average of €5 each).

Mobile phone - €19.95 - (It's a rolling sim only contract I can cancel at any time).

Socialising/sport - €291.20
- €100 - Alcohol/nights out (I'm not a big drinker, which helps).
- €191.20 - Meals out and other social activities such as concerts, cinema, or sports.

Public Transport - €20.80 - Public transport (Berlin is very bikeable, or this figure would be higher)

Total Variable Costs = €556.95

Fixed Costs (€767.89) + Variable Costs (€556.95) = Freedom Figure (€1324.84)

Before I came up with this system, I had the feeling that I knew how much money I spent each month, and where I spent it. However, only by recording my expenditure over several months did I realise how wrong I actually was about where my money went. It showed me precisely how much money I spent on unhealthy foods. How much was spent socialising. How much I gave to my local Asian restaurant. How much I spent on clothes. How much of my monthly financial commitment just disappeared in rent.

It's very much a truism that you can't optimise what you don't track. The Freedom Figure is the first step in this process. Once you know your expenditure, you can better decide if that expenditure is justified.

In my case, you can see that, every month, in order to break even and not diminish my savings, I need to earn €1324.84 after tax. (At an income of €16k per year there is very little tax to pay. If I earn more, I simply pay more tax, so it's of no great significance.) If I earn €100 more or spend €100 less in the month, my savings increase by €100. If the opposite is true, they decrease by €100. It's pretty much as simple as that.

I administer my finances from two separate accounts:

Income

Automatically paid
into this account

| 1. Savings Account (only online access, no debit card) | → | 2. Freedom Figure Account (normal online/debit card access) |

€1324.84 transferred by direct debit each month to Freedom Figure account.

Major Expenses
Made yearly when possible after calculating *Lifestyle Burn Rate*

Daily Expenses

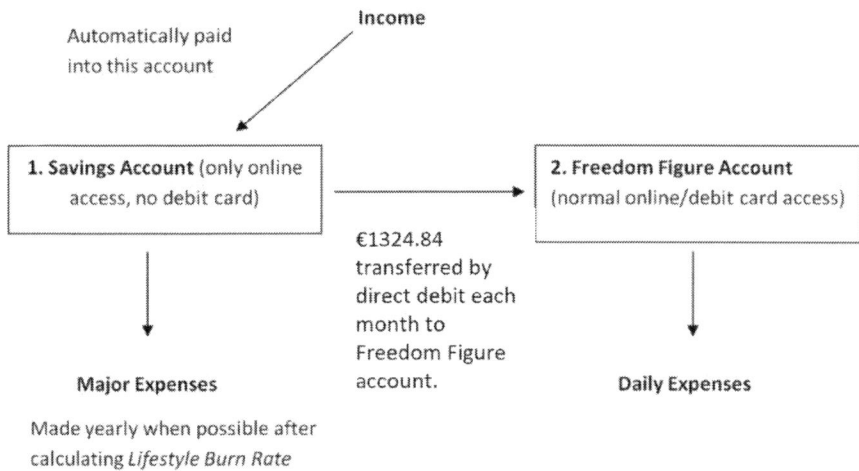

A savings account - All of my income goes directly into this account. I have online banking for it, but do not carry a debit card to access the money from it.

A Freedom Figure account - This is my daily current account. At the start of the month I have a standing order that transfers €1324.84 from my savings account into this account. It is from this money that I live each month.

I've been optimising my Freedom Figure for several years, so it's pretty lean by now. It could be lower than that, probably around €1100, but any less and I'm forced to make sacrifices in my quality of life. At €1324.84, I'm good. I know this because I've tested each component of my lifestyle. €1324.84 seems to be the sweet spot for my life in Berlin. It's where I'm living well, don't need to think about money, have all that I need, and am not making too many compromises.

Because of this system, I can see at any time in the month, at a glance, how much spending money I have left by checking the total in my current account. If I've gone a little crazy in the first few weeks, which almost never happens because my lifestyle is very, very stable by now, then I have to cut back a bit at the end. If I don't spend all of my Freedom Figure allowance each month, then it sits there and I have a bit more for decadences the following month. I also keep a list of personal R&D projects, books, courses, and other personal growth opportunities, which is an idea from Ramit Sethi's book *I Will Teach You to Be Rich*. I sometimes use extra cash to buy the things on this list. Or sometimes I just blow it all on booze and sweets. The choice is mine.

At this point, you're probably thinking *It's not that easy though, is it? Your system is far too simplistic. What about all that other stuff like car repairs, holidays, new clothes, trips to the dentist, and children? Will you not think about the children, Adam? Where are they in your Freedom Figure?*

Yes, of course it's not that easy. There are always minor fluctuations caused by unexpected expenses. Sometimes urgent costs come up from time to time, like repairing my bike, going to the dentist, or flying home because of a family emergency. Where possible, I pay for that stuff from my Freedom Figure account and try to adjust my lifestyle that month to absorb the cost—which is possible 9 times out of 10. When it is not possible because the bill is simply too large, sometimes, very, very reluctantly, I'm forced to transfer just enough from my savings account to plug the hole in my expenses created by this unforeseen cost. This makes me very sad, and so I do it only when forced, maybe once a year.

Otherwise, I make large purchases that are not urgent at the end of the year. Then I can look at my savings account and better decide whether or not it's grown enough over the course of the year to justify making a larger one-off purchase like a winter holiday or a new laptop, or how much money from the year I should move into my pension account. Since I already have more clothes than I need, I'll usually do a quick spree in the January sales and make sure I have enough to last me the rest of the year. If I decide to purchase a luxury item, it's only after first consulting my savings account. I also always pay for all major expenses at once, in full, since paying in installments is incompatible with my sporadic income.

For someone like me, who has not had a regular nine-to-five job for about seven years, I've mentally accepted that my income will fluctuate. As temporary, freelance, and self-employed work becomes ever increasingly the norm, the same will apply to more of you. Therefore, we need simple financial metrics to help us quickly evaluate our finances and make decisions from them about how much we need to work, and how much we can afford to earn. My income can fluctuate, by my expenditure cannot. The less control we have over when money comes in, the stricter the control must be about what goes out. That's why I think the Freedom Figure system is so useful.

Lifestyle Burn Rate

While it might seem as if there is no great barrier against repeatedly transferring from the savings account to plug holes in the Freedom Figure account, this is not so. Over time, you get emotionally attached to the figure in the savings account. It's really painful to see it decrease. The main reason I don't like to see it decrease is that I know it will affect something called my *Lifestyle Burn Rate.* Together with my Freedom Figure, these are the only two financial metrics I care about. They're my water and my air.

Lifestyle Burn Rate is so important because I really, really don't want to return to being full-time employed. I think it's largely an outdated idea—a throwback to our former days of physical labour. Now, because of the greater mental challenges of the type of work most of us do today, at best we can probably hope to do four hours of really productive work each day. However, since we're contracted to be there for eight, we then spend another four pushing email about, trying to look busy, and counting down the hours until we can go home.

For many people, the chance to do even four productive hours would be an improvement. Often, we're hired for a specific skill—marketing, staff management, writing, editing, selling, whatever it might be. At the beginning, we get to devote a lot of time to that talent, and we add value to the company because of it, filling a specific need that they have that caused them to hire us. But then, as time progresses, as employees we become saddled with the discontents of company life—meetings, email ping pong, staff management, writing reports no one reads but that we inherited from someone else who inherited them from someone else and so on all the way back to about the last economic ice age, when probably no one was reading them either.

It's like a lawyer who, wanting to give something back to society, decides to volunteer in a local soup kitchen for an hour a week. The lawyer feels better, for he is doing some good. The soup kitchen is also happy, since it has another pair of hands to help out. But, at the same time, because of the high hourly rate the lawyer could command for legal work, if he just did an extra billable hour of legal work and donated the money from that to the soup kitchen, the kitchen could hire 10 people at minimum wage to work an hour. Twenty hands instead of two. Often, in our day jobs, we end up a little like that lawyer—not doing high value work for our employers, but slogging away in soup kitchens of meetings, emails, reports, and office politics. We find there's less and less time being devoted to that specific skill we were hired for. Our enjoyment of the job decreases because of this, and, in the end, for many people, four hours of good, productive work would already be a great daily success.

I don't want to be in that situation. I sometimes actually have nightmares where I have a "real job," and I wake up sweating, looking at my alarm clock and panicking that I'm late for work. Those nightmares decrease once I know exactly how many months it would be before I'd need to return to the working world if I didn't earn a single cent more. And this is exactly what my *Lifestyle Burn Rate* shows me.

Using the Freedom Figure system, it's a very simple formula to calculate a *Lifestyle Burn Rate*:

Current Savings / Freedom Figure = *Lifestyle Burn Rate* (in number of months of freedom)

So, assuming I had €20k in my savings account, and my current Freedom Figure is €1324.84:

€20,000 / €1324.84 = 15.09 months of freedom.

To borrow a colloquial phrase, this is my "fuck you money"—the number of months until I would have to return to office work and employment. In my case, at my age, since I have no family to support, it's the only truly important measure of my financial health. In this example, I would have 15.09 months worth of it.

Now, the great thing about knowing these two is:

1. Every € I can lower my monthly Freedom Figure decreases my *Lifestyle Burn Rate*, which means more months of freedom.

2. Knowing exactly how long your savings can last you helps you decide what work projects you'll accept and what you'll reject.

You might decide you like the security or structure of being regularly employed. That's fine. Everyone is different, and the Freedom Figure is still useful to you because it can show you how much money you should be able to save each month (earnings after tax - Freedom Figure). If you are offered a promotion (as Steve was) or a new job, and you know your Freedom Figure and your Lifestyle Burn Rate, you're in a better position to make a decision. Is it worth taking on the additional responsibility for how much extra in savings per month/year? If you're already automatically saving each month at your current wage and have plenty put away, it might give you the confidence to say, *No, I'm in a good spot where I am, thanks, I don't need the extra hassle.*

Efficiency in Some Areas Allows for Inefficiency in Others

Because I'm committed to self-employment and have worked hard to get my Freedom Figure as low as possible, I know that, while I have to be frugal in certain areas of my life, I can be absolutely lavish in others. Assuming you are currently full-time employed, you are likely *cash-rich* but *time-poor*. That's your choice. Personally, I prefer being *time-rich* and *cash-poor,* above a basic level of lifestyle.

In my experience, above a certain comfort level, time is vastly more valuable than money. So while I'm forced to be efficient with my money, I have the luxury of being inefficient with time. I also don't think that time is equally valuable. I think time when you are young is worth much more than time when you are old. When you're young you are healthy and fearless, and have the lowest commitments (and so the most opportunities). Even if I have to work until 15 minutes before my death, I'll gladly do it. But my twenties *were*—and the rest of my thirties *are* going to be—a time for fun and experimentation. They are likely to be the best, most obligation-free years of my life. If it can be avoided in any way, I'm not going to spend them working—unless it's working on my own businesses, or on a project that I'm really excited about, and for which I'm the boss.

Once I know I have a year or so stashed away in my savings, I feel more confident in turning down work that I don't find interesting, and instead focus on having time for my friends, family, and interests. I don't just do things for the money anymore—well, unless the money is really, really good and will buy me much more time than I would need to invest in earning it. Using the Freedom Figure system, I can easily quantify that and decide. For example, I can work out my daily needs.

Freedom Figure €1324.84 / 30 days = €44.16 per day.

My lifestyle costs me €44.16 per day. So if I'm offered work at a €250 day rate (after tax, which, since this depends on income, means I usually just -30% to be safe), I can divide my day rate by my Freedom Figure Per Day:

Day Rate €250 / Freedom Figure Day Rate €44.16 = 5.6 days.

For every day I work on this project, I buy myself a week's freedom at my current spending level. That's might not be a bad deal, depending on the work. Jobs are not the enemy—bullshit jobs are. Work is not the enemy—work provides meaning. Bullshit work is the enemy. The easiest way to create the financial flexibility to turn down bullshit jobs is to need not very much money—to have a really low Freedom Figure, which allows you to build up savings, which lowers your Lifestyle Burn Rate, making your savings last longer.

That's not to say that I don't work very hard. I do. Just in phases. Like when I'm really excited about a project, or near a deadline. The goal is just that it is my decision. If the day feels like it's going to be a write-off, rather than sit at my desk miserable, I'd rather just write it off and go do something else. I tend to work harder in winter, when there are less distractions, so that I can work less in summer when Berlin presents me a hundred different, better reasons to be outside and away from my keyboard.

While living this way means that I can't spend lavishly, and so own little more than a laptop and some stories, my life is rich in many other ways. I can sleep in whenever I like. I can have long breakfasts that become long brunches that become long lunches that become mid-afternoon snacks, sitting around talking with friends. I can scribble notes for a million projects, ideas, books, and blog posts that I know I'll never actually bring to fruition. Since I only accept work I can do from any location, I'm free to visit my family in the UK whenever I want. Or I can sub-let my apartment in Berlin—usually even at a small profit—and go live in Argentina for a few months, like I did earlier this year; or Mexico, as I did last year; or Thailand, as I did the year before.

However, more than those big, exotic yearly highlights, I think living this way allows me to enjoy my day-to-day more. I don't get stressed or feel rushed when my train is late or a red light stops me on my way to somewhere. I have the freedom to sit on a weekday, in the park, knowing there is absolutely no reason to look at my watch, because I have almost all the time in the world. If I want to make a decision—about my finances, about whether to take on a new work project, or just what to do at the weekend—I have time to mull it over. This is important because studies have shown that humans are really bad at making decisions during times of scarcity. If we don't have the luxury of long-term planning because we've an urgent need—like finding the money to pay a credit card bill or finding a new job before we run out of our savings—that urgency makes us more likely to make a poor decision. We get tempted to borrow from the future to pay the debts of today. Sendhil Mullainathan, an economist at Harvard and co-author of the book *Scarcity: Why Having Too Little Means So Much*, has studied this phenomenon extensively:

"You borrow from tomorrow, and tomorrow you have less time than you have today…It's a very costly loan…It's as if you are fighting a fire, and someone hands you a bucket of water. You're going to take the bucket and fight the fire." But in that moment, under that pressure, we neither have the time nor mental capacity to think about what comes with that bucket of water. "When you look at payday loans, when you look at all these predatory lending products, they all have that feature going for them. They really are that bucket of water that helps you with the fire that you're fighting. They come with all these strings attached. But that's not what you're looking at in the moment.[59]"

So, many of us can get caught in a bad decision cycle—using our month's pay to clear our credit cards, then using the credit card all month again. Or borrowing a little to cover a shortfall at the end of the month, which means we start the next month with a shortfall, which only increases the odds we'll end it again with an even larger shortfall. The more we borrow, the more fees we pay, the more stress we have, and the greater the odds that we have to borrow further in an attempt to break the cycle. Those bad decisions are not always financial. In just the same way, if we don't create time to exercise, to sleep, or to prepare healthy food, we're also borrowing from our future health—a future that we'll have to spend on diets, doing sport, at the doctors, or off sick recovering from the bad decisions of today.

This is precisely what the Freedom Figure approach tries to tackle. We're trying to insulate ourselves from having to make bad, short-term decisions, and wasting energy and stress digging ourselves out of the holes that those decisions make for us.

Convinced? Let's look now at how you can calculate and optimise your Freedom Figure.

1. Calculating Your Freedom Figure

The first step is as simple as it sounds. You just have to record all of your expenses. Just spend like normal, without judgment. Forget you're even paying attention.

There are many online tools or smartphone apps for recording your finances, and after a while it becomes a fairly compulsive habit to enter them after paying for something. I record mine to a very granular level in my smartphone app (I've just presented a top-level overview in this chapter). I like to know exactly how much goes on chocolate, on fizzy drink, on beer, on cocktails, on takeaways.

After about three months of recording your expenditure, you'll have enough data to create your first monthly Freedom Figure, using an average of those months. Over time, the longer you record, the better a prediction that figure will be.

Now, at first, your Freedom Figure will probably be scarily high— infinitely larger than you would have imagined. Or it will just almost perfectly match your monthly wage. Don't worry about that. This is just the start of your optimisation process. It's likely that you've experienced lifestyle creep on and off for years, as you've slowly upgraded your lifestyle.

2. Lowering your Freedom Figure

With your current Freedom Figure established, the fun can really begin, as you can begin experimenting to try and reduce it. Do you really need to spend €80 a month on the gym? Could you downgrade from two Starbucks coffee's a day to just one? How much would that save? You can try some of the monthly Lents that we discussed back in the chapter on expectations. I try a different Lent challenge each month—it might be home-cooking month, no-alcohol month, no-sugar month, no public transport, etc.

Your goal is to go through every one of your costs and work out if you could lower it or remove it altogether, without decreasing your lifestyle noticeably. After several months, you be able to reduce your Freedom Figure by at least 30%, much more if you can be convinced to move to a cheaper apartment, or gave up some other big expense, like a car. From there, you just have to keep chipping away, and who knows where you'll end up. What's important is just slow and steady positive progress. Remember, at no point should you consider your income in any of your decisions. It's not relevant at this stage.

It's also addictive to think about what would happen to your Freedom Figure if you were to move somewhere else. Since rent or your mortgage payment is likely to be the far largest of your monthly costs, reducing this one number is likely to have the largest impact on your Freedom Figures. Another city, another country, another apartment—it sounds drastic at first, I know, but just let the idea settle.

Technology, like the Internet, is significantly affecting the *where* and the *how* of work. It's becoming ever more realistic that, just as I have, you can find a job where you can work remotely. Or that you can start your own small company offering something online, as we'll discuss in later chapters. Your customers need never know, nor will they care, where you are based and how laughably low your cost of living is while you do their work. If you choose to, you can earn in €'s and live in Indian rupees or Thai baht. While your income will stay the same, your Freedom Figure might drop overnight to one half or one third of what it is now. This is the reason I live in Berlin. Having travelled on and off for years, I've found no city that offers as high a standard of living for such little money. Although I love it more than any place on earth, that's actually of secondary importance to me at this point. Within reason, I'm here for economic reasons. If it continues its rampant gentrification, there's a good chance I'll leave it in four or five years as it gets too expensive for someone who wants to live my kind of lifestyle.

Personally, I'd rather live in a cheap city and have time to work on my books or my websites than live in an expensive one and have to work for someone else eight hours each day, always worrying about being able to pay rent. "Fear inhibits innovation. In expensive cities, people live in constant fear. A small wrong move can upend everything, so they conform, terrified of losing their jobs, apartments, health insurance. They conform intellectually, and they conform in behaviour,[60]" says journalist Sarah Kendzior, who writes regularly about the "prestige economy" and how Millennials are being pushed into subservience by the so-called prestige of a university degree or internship at a major company.

Of course, it might be different for you. Perhaps paying Munich, New York, or London rents is totally justified based on what you receive. You're probably also very attached to the friends you have there and the community you are part of. That's fine. It all depends on what you value, and if those values have been put to the test so that they are more than just assumptions.

Not All €'s Are Equal

For people who can't save—like my financially reckless friend— every € spent each month up to their Freedom Figure is likely to be the most valuable. They're paying for the fundamentals of life. They're the difference between sleeping on the street and having an apartment; having a cold apartment or a heated apartment; being hungry or having enough food to eat; walking to work in the rain or taking the bus. I think that life quality is a lot like product quality. Up to a certain point, when it comes to what we buy, the more we pay, the more we receive. But at roughly our Freedom Figure, that begins to change.

Unless we're disciplined savers, it's likely that every € we spend above our Freedom Figure each month—even if we've never heard of the concept or calculated it—is likely being frittered away on luxuries that are not meaningfully adding to our monthly happiness. Unless we've great imagination about what to do with our post-Freedom Figure money—which most of us don't—we're likely to just unnecessarily upgrade myriad small daily purchases decisions (whether it's upgrading from the basic, shabby Asian restaurant on the street corner where we used to eat twice a week to the fancier one next door for twice the price, swapping the old €50 bag we've happily carried for a year for a new €150 designer version, selling our two-generation-old smartphone for the slightly newer, slimmer one with a new blue light on the top, or upgrading from that four-zone mattress to the eight-zone lumbar support memory foam mattress). It's very easy to be led around by our incomes, letting our lifestyles swell accordingly. We all like to splurge sometimes.

That's fine. But it's better to have a low cost of living and splurge occasionally, than to have a high cost of living and be unconsciously splurging every month; confusing things we want with the things we need; confusing quality with price, which is really easy to do. A nice test is to go to the supermarket and pick a food item. It can be pretty much anything—chocolate bars, barbeque crisps, fish fingers, wine—and buy three of it: the absolute cheapest, a middle priced option, and the most expensive. Then do a blind taste test. See which wins. See if you think the price difference charged for each is justified.

In Conclusion

It's easy to think that we've consciously made the important decisions in our lives—that we've designed our lifestyles, and not had them designed for us by our incomes. An easy way we can know for sure what we *need* (rather than what we *want* and what we've merely *become used to*), is the Freedom Figure, since it requires us to quantify the exact cost of our desired lifestyles, and challenges us to reduce it slowly, divorcing income from expenditure to help us fight against lifestyle creep.

Much of the advice in the rest of this book is going to involve major life upheavals of the big and scary variety. If we follow it, a reliable income is about to become a thing of the past for us, assuming market forces have not already rendered it so. The more savings we have stashed away, the better. The lower we can get our Freedom Figures, the better. Think of savings like *failure insurance,* or financial security blankets. It's going to take some time to get to where we are going, and there will be more wrong turns than a maze of mirrors. Savings and a low cost of living are what will keep us on track.

Case Study - Emma Barnie aka The Bowl's Club Squatter

In preparation for this chapter I asked around for who knew someone who seemed particularly happy, yet had very little. One name came up again and again: Barnie. Different friends would tell me their favourite Barnie legends until she became a kind of *Kaiser Sosay* figure, only for lean living. "Barnie lives almost without money," one would say. "Barnie has gold bars in a bank vault," another would add. "Barnie lives in a squat in London that's nicer than your house." "Barnie only eats food from dumpsters."

Finally, after a few failed attempts and the world's most disjointed SMS conversation, I met Barnie outside Balham tube station, in south London. Barnie was wearing a loose blue shirt with flowers, a blue skirt, and shin blue leggings—a look I'd describe as hippie casual. She invited me back to her squat. My first ever squat, in fact. Having walked just a couple of streets from the station, we then turned down an unpaved side street. At the end of that street was a lilac wooden door. Barnie got out her key and unlocked it, just like you might any other door. It was slightly anti-climactic. I was expecting more stealth—fence climbing, hiding from security guards, baiting wild dogs with steaks. Instead, she turned that key, we entered, and I was confronted with a massive green garden— possibly the largest private garden I've ever seen. And in London, no less. It turned out Barnie was squatting in an old Lawn Bowl's clubhouse. I'd estimate her garden to be almost exactly the size of a bowl's pitch.

The squat is comprised of three rooms, one large room that used to be the main clubhouse, with beautiful wooden beams, alternately painted black and white, and two rooms now being used as bedrooms. They're all mostly filled with junk—clothing, old furniture, CDs, books, and puzzles. It's like a cross between a flea market and the end of the world. In the main room live two of

Barnie's roommates—one behind a giant sheet of plastic, and another upstairs on a homemade big wooden plank accessed by a makeshift ladder.

Off the main room is the bathroom. It's not so bad, and the toilet's flush works from collected rainwater, which England no doubt offers them in spades. There's even a bath. It's plastic, and extremely practical being as it is strategically located below a large hole in the roof, so the rain drops directly into it. Barnie and Nick's room is big, around 25sqm, in an L shape. Nick has the bottom of the L, Barnie the top. There's no sound protection, no walls, just a corner to separate them, a few more holes in the roof, and a very dusty piano. Could I live here? I doubt it. I doubt it very much.

Over a pleasant few hours in this garden, Barnie tells me about her life. It all started when she travelled Europe in a camper van with an old boyfriend, and found she liked the lifestyle. She was a little surprised herself that she didn't miss the luxuries of a real home. After returning from that trip—and out of money—she tried squatting and eventually lucked into the Bowl's club squat. Even though it has no running water, heating, or electricity, she found living in it was not so bad. Not all the urban legends surrounding her were true, though. While she used to live almost completely without money, these days she's been less strict with herself. She even has a cash-in-hand job as an artist's assistant. She now rarely eats from dumpsters, although she used too, before the supermarkets nearby upgraded their security to try and keep her and her co-squatters out. The rumours about her having gold in the bank turn out to be true, though. It was the advice of a friend who assured her gold never loses value. She still travels for months a year, hitchhiking and accessing a kind of thrifty underground squatter network I didn't even know existed, and that is apparently full of people sharing tips, tricks, and resources for how to live on the cheap. It's clear that it's a sort of challenge to her, to see how little she can live on, and on how few people she can depend.

I tried to push Barnie on her opinions. I really wanted her to chastise the Londoners around her working nine to five and paying hundreds, or more likely thousands a month in rent or on mortgages, while she paid precisely €0. I wanted her to call these people "sheeple" and "idiots" and "chumps." I wanted her to quote Marx at me and call me a corporate sell out. But she did none of these things. "I think that's fine, if that's what they want," was all the scorn she could muster for the full-time employed. At first I was disappointed. I thought that maybe her views were not provocative enough to be included in this book. But now, having written so much of it, I see that what she's doing is even more relevant *because* of how normal she is. Extremes are interesting, at first glance, but often so far from our own lives that they're hard to relate. I think it's just off normal, therefore, that's probably the most interesting or actionable for us in our everyday lives. *People like Barnie.* She's living the Freedom Figure lifestyle, just taken to its extreme. She's making rational decisions about how to structure her life. She's not opting out—she's still in the system, she's just not fully in. She's systematically attacked her cost of living and how low she can get her Freedom Figure (currently around €200). She's testing what she can remove from her life and still be happy. Knowing that she is perfectly comfortable living in a chaotic environment like a squat, without running water and electricity, it makes no sense to pay London rents. Knowing how little money she needs, and that she prefers to be time-rich and cash-poor, why should she work any longer than necessary? If there's a perfectly good building that no one else is using, why should she not use it? Of course, our definition of perfectly good is unlikely to be the same as hers, but hers has been tested in a way that ours probably hasn't.

Knowing that we're wired to experience loss much more acutely than gain, it's important that we don't rush to add things to our lives with no regard for their sustainability or the pain we'll feel should we have to remove them. It's very easy to bumble along, believing you're making decisions when really they're making you—living life by default, to borrow a phrase from author David Cain, who wrote a hugely popular essay on the topic. "It is typical for the major aspects of a human life (career, friends, habits and home) to be decided by happenstance, and not consciously. The feeling of something huge being missing is probably often due to a serious mismatch between what you currently have in one of those aspects, and what is best for you in one of those aspects."

This is something that's hard for us to accept, because we like to believe that we have chosen the important parts of our lives—our jobs, our cities, our countries, our partners, our friends—when in reality we're often just following previous decisions made at earlier points in time, when we knew neither ourselves nor our options as well as we do today. So we live where we studied. We're friends with our colleagues, or ex-colleagues, not because they're suited to us but because we spend all day with them. We live in the country where we grew up, regardless of how hard it might be to make a living there. "Few people make a deliberate quest out of finding their perfect city or neighborhood, of seeking out truly like-minded people. Most of us live 70 or 80 years defending what we've been given, because we think it's who we are," says David. I like that Barnie is so committed to *not* doing this.

Part 3 – Act.

It's now time to put all that we've learned thus far into practice. While opportunity might work a little bit differently in the digital age, there's certainly no less of it. While the world is getting harder for people who want to take direction, it's never been more open and available for those of us willing to be flexible and create our own opportunities. Anyone can flourish in the digital age, and the next four chapters are devoted to showing you how.

"Everyone thinks of changing the world, but no one thinks of changing himself." — Leo Tolstoy

Chapter 10 - Become the Best Marketer

You probably noticed a long time ago that the world is not fair, so it is completely redundant for me to bother pointing it out. Stupidly, I used to think that it was fair. I wasn't totally naïve—I knew that we didn't all have the same opportunities or material comforts. But I thought that somehow this must be compensated for in another way that was not immediately obvious—that there were probably some higher cosmic guardians of karma who were keeping tally and regulating score, evening out wrong doings, punishing the unjust, etc. While you lost out in some areas, you gained in others.

I've now travelled to enough of the world to know how spectacularly wrong that was.

There is no equality, no justice, no karma. No higher power is watching. No one is going to intervene. There's no relationship between effort and reward, talent and success. Maybe unfair is not even the right word to describe it all. Life is not exactly *unfair*, it's just *indifferent*. It's not choosing the losers or winners. It's simply not paying attention. It's perfectly happy to tolerate the simultaneous existence of both billionaires and paupers, triathletes and cripples, radical Muslims and militant atheists, capitalism and communism, workaholics and sloths, alcoholics and teetotalers, Hanukahs and holocausts.

With all that said, the fact that we are here—with the luxury of the time, ability, and desire to read these words—means we're probably already a proud, non-card-carrying member of humanity's richest five percent. The five percent that has a roof over its head, access to clean water, the ability to read and write, and a job. Even though it was probably, mostly, down to a completely arbitrary accident of birth, we are still winning at life.

If the world were truly fair, however, opportunities would not be distributed so haphazardly. They'd go to the most deserving, the most talented, and the hardest working. I'm not sure about you, but I know that wouldn't be lazy, fickle me. If the world's not fair, though, we don't need to be the best. We don't need to work harder than our competitors. We don't need to be nice or fair. Of course, we can choose to be if we want, but that's entirely up to us. We can't expect any reward for that, unless we give ourselves that reward. Maybe we find we can sleep better at night, or are able to hold our heads that little bit higher as we walk through our days, safe in the knowledge that we did the right thing (as we so chose to define it).

If the world is not fair, we don't need to memorize the whole route. We can just find the shortcuts, the exceptions, the places where all the overlapping, complex systems that comprise life create a small gap of prosperity just wide enough for us to sneak through. In my experience, the biggest shortcut is *marketing*.

Looking around, I see many people still behaving as if the world is fair. These are people who plug away, day after day, quietly perfecting their craft, believing that, if they keep working hard, they are going to get discovered. That their talent, skill, knowledge, and experience is going to be rewarded. *That today is going to be their day.*

Only that day never comes. They never get their big break. I think that a mixture of Hollywood, religion, our parents, and the media are all, to varying degrees, complicit in spreading the myth that talent and hard work will be rewarded with success. But sadly, for every success story, there are 999 almost identical people, perhaps smarter, more dedicated, more talented than those who broke through, and yet are left toiling away in complete isolation, unrecognised and unpaid.

Because, unfortunately, life is not a perfectly calibrated machine in which talent and hard work are poured in and the requisite amount of success drops neatly out of the bottom. Marketing is one of the ways that you recalibrate it. It allows you to steal, buy, generate, and redirect attention.

In an unfair world, it's not the most talented that rise to the top, but the best marketers.

There simply is no absolute impartial measure of quality. No scale. Like the Richter scale, only for talent. Quality is in the eye (and ears) of the beholder. McDonalds, Coca-Cola, Budweiser, reality TV, Paris Hilton, the wages of professional football players, the movies of Adam Sandler or Vin Diesel—all, in my humble opinion, further examples of the power of marketing and distribution over actual talent and quality—quality that is completely irrelevant anyway if no one finds the thing to be appraised in the first place, because it is too badly marketed.

I call this *Gangnam's Law*. Gangnam's Law states that the popularity of something is more likely explained by its marketing than by its quality. It is, of course, named after the hit song/video Gangnam Style in which a man dances by pretending he's riding a horse, whilst singing largely inaudible words. It's an artistic feat so outstanding it's been viewed more than two billion times on YouTube alone. At four minutes a song, that's an investment of more than 16,000 years of humanity's time, approximately one and a half times as long as we invested creating all of Wikipedia.

While it's always tempting to focus with exclusion on *the thing you can do*, it's very often *how people are going to find out about the thing you do* that matters much more, especially in an unfair, Gangnam world. Thriving in the digital age is about both understanding this and being willing to use it to your advantage.

Busk, don't beg

Every few weeks, I read a depressing article in an English newspaper about an unemployed graduate who, despite all his best efforts, just can't find work. The article will begin with some wider statistics about the increasing number of graduates leaving university and failing to find graduate level work, and how the average student debt is also at a record high. Then it will focus on the story of one specific graduate. This graduate will be photographed sitting in front of his laptop, looking exacerbated. Next to them will be a large stack of paper, which is usually supposed to represent all the applications they've written, even though most likely they've sent them digitally. The article will tell us the exact number of jobs they've applied for. It will be more than 100, sometimes several hundred. The graduate will be quoted saying something like, "It's really frustrating. I'm not sure what I'm doing wrong. No one is willing to give me a chance."

I always feel very sorry for this person. So much so that I wanted to write this book to try and help them understand why they are often doing everything their peers tell them, everything previous generations did, and yet they're not getting the same results.

However, mostly when I read those articles, I think about Einstein's famous quote: "The definition of stupidity is doing the same thing multiple times yet expecting different results."

If you are that graduate and you've sent out a hundred applications and still not got a job—and maybe just a few interviews—logically, the solution is not to crack on with the 101st application. If it didn't work the past hundred times, it's not likely to this time. There must be something fundamentally wrong with your approach—something that sitting at home and scatter-gunning out yet more CVs and copy-pasted cover letters—to people you've never met, spoken to, or demonstrated your skills to, asking them to employ you—is ever going to solve.

What's changed in the digital age?

I think that opportunity works a little bit differently in the digital age, and this partly explains why graduates are struggling. It is directly related to the *don't be the best, be the best marketer* advice of the previous chapter. Before the Internet, there was no direct, easy, egalitarian, digital link between three billion people. If information needed to spread, it relied on certain gatekeepers to propagate it—gatekeepers like newspapers or television.

Let's take book publishing as a practical example. Pre-Internet, if we wanted to publish a book, we could write it. That part was not a problem—we could just use regular old analogue pen and paper if we wanted. *No gatekeepers.* But when we wanted to find readers for it, then we hit a wall. We could stand on the street and wave our manuscript in passing people's faces, but that wouldn't scale very well and would make our arms ache. Remember, no Internet means no Amazon, and so no e-commerce. So we couldn't sell our book online. Pre-Internet, if people wanted to buy a book, they probably went to a bookstore to find one. So our book needs to be in bookstores, next to all the other books.

We've found your first gatekeeper: *bookstores.*

Now, we can't just approach these bookstores directly. There are not enough hours in the day for them to negotiate with every would-be author like us. No, they just buy their books from a few dozen different publishers, to keep things simple.

We've found our next gatekeeper: *book publishers.*

We have to approach one of these few dozen publishers and convince them it's in their financial interest to release our book and pass it on to bookstores on our behalf. In the same way bookstores don't have time to deal with every single would-be author, publishers don't either. We could try sending our manuscript directly to them, unsolicited, but many people do that, and so it'll probably just end up as part of a giant slush pile of unsolicited manuscripts, in a dark musty corner of an intern's office, never to be read by anyone. So our best bet becomes finding a literary agent to represent it. Agents have an in with the publishers and so can get it read by them.

We've found our third gatekeeper: *agents.*

Between us and our legion of potential happy readers now sits three gatekeepers who all need to be convinced of our book before it can reach the masses. Not only do we need to convince them, we need to pay them a cut of every sale.

Pre-Internet, gatekeepers were a big problem.

Even if we created a truly great product or service, it was hard to reach our potential customers with it, because gatekeepers sat in the way. This was what was so exciting and revolutionary about the Internet—it was truly egalitarian (at least at first—we could debate what it has become today)—and so everyone would finally have a voice. We would create something truly participatory. A stay-at-home mum of two's blog could compete directly with the *New York Times.* Anyone could find an audience for their poetry, music, products, books, ideas, or cat pictures.

Everyone would be equal on the Internet! Down with gatekeepers!

For a while, this worked quite well. We did remove many gatekeepers. In the world of publishing, Amazon came along with their Kindle e-reader and kick started self-publishing for the masses. Today, anyone can self-publish their book. Amazon is a gatekeeper, but a very slutty one. They will accept almost any submission. We can upload a book of crayon-illustrated unicorn poetry and they'll let us at least try and sell it. E-commerce has helped destroy gatekeepers, letting more and more products out and liberating the so-called "long tail" of commerce.

As a result, the traditional gatekeepers of publishing—publishers, agents, and bookstores—are slowly losing power, for they no longer control the big literary gate that connects readers to writers. The Internet and self-publishing has opened it up, and all are free to pass without paying the tolls that previously existed. In the words of Clay Shirky, what happened was that publishing experienced a "mass amateurisation." Gatekeepers were removed, and we replaced the economic output of a smaller number of experts with an explosion of amateurs.

But what was harder to foresee in this happy, new, digital utopia is that if you give everyone a voice, how the hell is anyone going to get heard? If everyone is broadcasting, how can we attract people to our frequency and convince them we are worth listening to? How can we ensure the best stuff does rise to the top? How can we hide all the crayon-drawn unicorn poetry?

Logically, the more people creating, contributing, selling, and passing through the wide-open gates of literature, manuscript in hand, the more competition there is on the other side of that gate. The Internet swapped the distribution problem for a new problem—*discovery*.

Everything is now available, but almost nothing gets found.

In many ways it's quite similar to the gatekeeper problem, only now the gatekeepers are our time and attention spans.

Now, let's get back to that poor graduate at home, writing cover letters and sending out their CV. The Internet has changed recruitment in just the same way as it has changed publishing. Depending on the specialisation of the job, if a company needs someone with a certain skill, they can just Google that skill + *city name* and see who turns up, and contact them directly. They don't need to wait for an application. They can go to Linkedin or Xing and search a database of millions for someone with the unique blend of the skills they want. They can look up who is doing the job at their competitor's and poach them directly. They can hire via a recommendation of their employees. They can hire a contractor or a freelancer via a recruitment firm. They can outsource their jobs to a remote worker in a different country willing to work for far less money.

Just as the bookstore and publishers didn't have time to deal with the legions of would-be authors who want to sell there, many companies today don't have time to sort the application *wheat* from the application *chaff*, and so many outsource the task to a motley mix of head hunters, recruitment agents, and personal recommendations from their existing staff.

Of course, they won't all do these things, and for many jobs it would make no sense to—just as it doesn't make sense for everyone to self-publish. But for increasing amounts of people, it will.

Graduates can still sit at home and churn out CVs and cover letters, but if everyone else is doing that, as soon as they have to compete against someone with better grades, more experience, or a willingness to work for less money, they're out. The barriers to applying are so low that long gone are the days when you heard about a job from a friend of a friend, or had to wait and cut out an ad from the local newspaper. It's all online, and on one of a few major job portals that everyone else is also checking. Just like in self-publishing, graduates job hunting are competing against more and more people for the attention of would-be employers. The longer this goes on, the harder it gets. The longer we're out of work, the less likely it is that someone is going to take a chance on us, purely because no one else has taken a chance on us. They assume we must be defective in some way. It's like finding a book on Amazon released in 2011 that has no reviews. It seems suspicious.

How do we get out of this situation? How do we improve our odds? How do we get discovered?

We have to change our approach. Like the Bible, like the movies of Adam Sandler, like Gangnam Style, we have to become the best marketer. We have to find a way to separate ourselves from the masses, and to demonstrate what we can do. If the world was fair, we wouldn't have to—people would see all we have to offer. But it's not. We have to *busk*, not *beg* for an opportunity.

Busk, don't Beg

In 2010, copywriter Alec Brownstein, just like the graduate from the start of this chapter, found himself unemployed. He knew he wanted to work for one of a handful of top digital agencies in New York, but that they probably received hundreds of applications every month. So he knew he'd need an unusual way of approaching them in order to get their attention. What he did was simple, but ingenious. Instead of just sending off a CV and cover letter and crossing his fingers, he made a simple one-page website and purchased Google Adwords ads (a kind of sponsored search result that we'll discuss later). He paid so that these ads would appear when someone Googled the name of one of the six executives that headed the agencies he wanted to work for. He suspected that these six individuals would probably Google themselves from time to time to see what people had written about them, so he created an ad for each of the six that simply said, "Hey, *executive's name*—Googling yourself is a lot of fun. Hiring me is fun, too."

This was an incredibly smart but simple idea. In total, Alec spent $6 on these Google ads. His hunch regarding executive vanity proved correct. As a result of his ads, he was contacted and interviewed by four of the six executives whom he tried to reach. From those four interviews, he got two job offers. He accepted one and got his dream job.

While this was a really smart idea, it's no surprise or fluke that it worked. He was applying to digital agencies, after all. Their job is to create smart digital content that gets attention, just as his ads did. Rather than *begging* for a chance of a job armed with nothing more than his CV and the promise that he knew what we was doing, he proved it by *busking*, demonstrating all the skills they were looking for. With a great idea, and $6, he created something so sticky that people like me, years later, are still talking about it. That's exactly the sort of thing the clients of the agencies he was applying to want for their business, so it's no surprise that he got a job.

Another similar example is Andrew Horner, who, in 2010, two years out of college, found himself still out of work. "No employer would give my resume a second glance, no human resources manager would line up an interview for me; even the recruiters were slow to return my calls...I knew my talents would be an excellent addition to virtually any business, but the entire job-seeking process had eaten away at every shred of self-confidence I once possessed."

His solution was something called the *Reverse Job Application* (you can still find it online at http://www.reversejobapplication.com/). Rather than apply to companies, he made a website that showcased all of his skills and charm, and invited companies to *apply to him* for the chance of his employment. He literally reversed the normal job application process, hence the name.

Listing his skills, such as being "a leader in inexperienced professionalism. My years of unemployment have given me many opportunities to avoid picking up bad habits from your competitors," he turned every negative that he had into a positive, and in the process flipped his position from one of weakness (sending out CVs and covering letters) to one of strength. He went from *push* to *pull*, demonstrating all of the reasons that he should be hired in the first place (his IT skills, his creativity, his flair for words, his ability to generate press attention).

As with Alec Brownstein's Google ads, all Andrew Horner did was create one simple, single-page website. He had the confidence to *busk, not beg* for an opportunity. It's far easier to convince people of your worth when you're showing them what you've already done, rather than what you want their permission to let you do.

I think these two examples perfectly encapsulate how opportunities are being distributed in the digital age, and the importance of getting out there and busking your skills to get them. What you know doesn't really matter anymore. Proving how you can use everything that you know to add value to your employer is what matters.

Case Study - The Good in Bad Ideas

The popular rhetoric is that ideas come in two forms—*good* and *bad*. Good ideas are easy to spot, because they belong to successful people, products, businesses and services. Bad ideas are equally easy to spot because they belong to unsuccessful people, products, businesses, and services. Our measure of whether an idea is good is usually based on whether the idea worked or not, rather than the actual idea itself. Confirmation bias in action. We accept evidence that confirms our hunches, and disregard what doesn't. We forget about all the myriad hidden factors that decide why something might succeed or fail (as we already discussed back in Chapter 5)—effort, talent, money, luck, execution, timing, and marketing. Mostly, marketing. A brilliant idea in the hands of an incompetent person is worth much less than a shitty idea in the hands of a brilliant marketer. Here are some more examples of the thin line between good and bad, stupidity and genius, and the power of novelty to attract attention, the scarcity of our times:

Iwanttodrawacatforyou.com - A real service, where, since 2011, more than 15,000 people have paid $9.95 to get a single black and white picture of a cat drawn by a man called Paul. It works precisely because it shouldn't work. Because it's a bad idea, but an entertaining, little bit stupid one. The site got its big break on flash sale site Groupon where it sold the first thousand pictures, and snowballed from there.

Somethingstore.com - A website where you spend $10 and receive a something. You have no idea what it is until it arrives. You can't influence what it is in any way. Terrible idea. Great business. 221,757 people have bought a something since it started in 2008. That's more than two million dollars in revenue.

Kashiwa Mystery Cafe - Flying in direct contrast to "the customer is always right," this Japanese restaurant's gimmick is that you don't receive what you order, but *what the person before you ordered.* What you order goes to the next customer. Only good at cooking one dish? No problem. In Cambodia I heard of a restaurant where they've only one dish, a family recipe they've cooked every day for the past 20-odd years.

Somebody Please Take Pity and Give Me a Job - In 2014, Dave Robins, a 36-year-old Welsh man found himself unemployed. He claims to have applied to more than a thousand jobs, getting just two responses. So, just like I'm advising, he decided to do something different. He made an eBay auction called *Somebody Please Take Pity and Give Me a Job* and offered to sell a week of his labour to the highest bidder, doing whatever work they wanted. Unfortunately, the winning bid was £10.50. However, the media then discovered him, he listed himself again for another week and, amazingly, the second time his services fetched £8,300.

Zach "Danger" Brown's Potato Salad - In 2014, Ohio native Zach Brown wrote a funny Kickstarter post asking for just $10 to make some potato salad. Much to humanity's surprise, his funny campaign went viral, precisely because it was so funny, stupid, and simple, and because he asked for such a small amount of money compared to most crowdfounding campaigns. It spread via social networking sites like Reddit, and he ended up raising $55,000, much of which he spent on a big potato salad festival called PotatoStock.

Tom's Shoes - Tom's make shoes. Simple, understated shoes sold at high prices. These high prices are because every time you buy a pair of Tom's shoes, they give another pair to a child in need. Since 2006, they've donated more than 35 million pairs. Charity through capitalism. Redemption through consumption. It's pretty illogical, in my opinion. But just like all these examples, it works not because we are buying a pair of shoes, or a potato salad, or a cat picture, but because we're buying the story that we can tell about how we acquired that pair of shoes, the potato salad, or that cat picture. In the end, the anecdote, the experience, is more important than anything else. There is (almost) no such thing as a bad idea, just a badly marketed idea.

"Losers have goals. Winners have systems." – Scott Adams, creator of Dilbert.

Chapter 12 - Trust in Systems, not Goals

In 2009, after living in New Zealand for a year, my girlfriend and I were on our way back to Europe, and stopped over in Japan for a few weeks. As a technology enthusiast I'd always wanted to see the neon lights of Tokyo and to sleep in a capsule hotel, and randomly push buttons on a fancy space age toilet. However, the first thing we discovered about Tokyo, whilst attempting to locate said capsule hotel, is that while Tokyo might be technologically superior in many areas, it really struggles with the urban basics, like logical city planning.

Attempting to find a specific address in Tokyo involves finding four different numbers: one for area, sub-area, block, and house complex. That sounds simple, but since there is no central planning and many areas are really just older areas that have been subdivided, the numbers are not assigned sequentially. So you're walking along past blocks 6 and 7, fully expecting the next block to be block 8, the block you need, only to be presented with block 17, followed by block 12. You can ask people for help, but it turns out they have no idea where anything is either.

At first this was quite frustrating, since we'd taken the time to research a number of specific strange attractions that we were sure would reveal to us something poignant about Japanese culture—a love hotel with a dungeon-themed room, the world's biggest Manga shop, or a restaurant themed like a mental hospital. Unfortunately, only about half the time we set out to find one of these curious attractions did we *actually find one of these curious attractions*.

After a few days of traipsing around the city like this, we realised that each time we went out to find something specific, even though we only found them 50 percent of the time, it didn't really matter. What we found on the way, by accident and happenstance, was always really interesting, probably even more so than what we were actually looking for in the first place. A church-theme bar, in which we could drink neon cocktails from severed dolls' heads whilst sitting under a giant crucified Jesus. A baseball pitch in the middle of a housing complex where we spectacularly failed to hit baseballs fired at us by pitching machines. A sex shop where they sold used fast food restaurant outfits and soiled underwear. An empty Beatles-themed bar hidden away in a basement.

Having a target was just a nice way to get us out of the hotel and push us in a certain direction and into a new area of the city where the gods of serendipity would then reward our geographic bravery by presenting us something completely ridiculous to enjoy.

I think this is similar to how opportunities work in an unfair, unjust, random world, and it builds on everything we've covered in the past two chapters. Of course, it's very tempting to create a specific goal for ourselves and our lives—a some concrete aim, just as my girlfriend and I did in Japan. That goal might be running a marathon, becoming a published author, working for Google, climbing Everest, or retiring at 30 to that island shaped like our face. The problem is that if the finish line is well marked, it's very obvious and very painful for us all of the time that we haven't reached it. Not only that, but our determination and fixation upon it may leaves us less likely to notice, or willing to explore, interesting-looking side streets that present themselves along the way.

Goals are nice, but they can be too prescriptive and inflexible for how the world actually works and how little of it actually lies within our control. This was articulated best by Scott Adams, creator of *Dilbert*, in his book How to Fail at Almost Everything and Still Win Big:

"If your goal is to lose 10 pounds, you will spend every moment until you reach the goal—if you reach it at all—feeling as if you were short of your goal. In other words, goal-oriented people exist in a state of nearly continuous failure that they hope will be temporary. If you achieve your goal, you celebrate and feel terrific, but only until you realize that you just lost the thing that gave you purpose and direction."

The solution, suggested by Scott, is to create systems, not goals. Systems are more understanding of *failure*, because they have a less prescriptive, fixed view of what constitutes *success*. After all, as clichéd as it might be, it really is the journey and not the destination that counts. By following a system, we can celebrate every small step of incremental progress on that journey, regardless of whether we have reached any idealised destination. While we won't necessarily know exactly where we are going, we can relax and enjoy the ride, safe in the knowledge that we are getting better at whatever it is we are doing—painting, writing, programming, growing a business, etc.

Systems push us in the right general direction, while not specifying the exact route we should take to get there. Which I think fits better in a world that is not fair, and in which talent is simply not enough to guarantee success. The system forces us out there, marketing ourselves, busking our skills to the masses, without telling us where we'll end up. As Scott said about starting *Dilbert*, his big hit, "...every day during those years I woke up with the same thought, literally, as I rubbed the sleep from my eyes and slapped the alarm clock off...*Today's the day*. If you drill down on any success story, you always discover that luck was a huge part of it. You can make it easier for luck to find you. The most useful thing you can do is stay in the game. The universe has plenty of luck to go around; you just need to keep your hand raised until it's your turn. It helps to see failure as a road and not a wall.[61]"

Everyone has something they can do well—something they find easier than other people; something they can offer that other humans might potentially need. We all speak at least one language fluently, a language that someone somewhere wants to learn. We all have at least one specialist topic that we can talk to people about for hours, because we're very knowledgeable and passionate about it. There is no shortage of ideas. No shortage of opportunities. No well-defined, well-trodden, well-sign-posted route to success. The most important thing is just that we start. Start walking. Start running. Start a blog. Start a business. Start a club. Join a club. *Just start*.

Get out there and busk. Design a system that lets you practice that skill each day. Get slowly better at it, and at sharing it. Like lost tourists in Tokyo, who knows what weird and interesting places following your talent will take you.

There is no shortage of opportunities, just an opportunity distribution problem.

I'm a very hairy man. I'm the sort of hairy man that even hairy men would describe as *hairy*. I would guess, by conservative estimates, that approximately 90% of my body is covered in a dense blanket of hair. Ironically, the largest hair-free part of me is the top of my head. For, like many hairy men, in my late twenties, I went bald. Now, people observing just the top of my head might conclude that I have a shortage of hair. That I, in fact, have a *hair problem*. But this is like guessing the size of the iceberg based only on what is above the waterline.

I don't have a hair problem—I have a *hair distribution problem*.

I think that, in just the same way, when people complain of a lack of opportunities, what they really mean is there is *an opportunity distribution problem*.

Because the world is a giant, unfair, random, indifferent, clusterfuck of happenstance, it's perhaps no surprise that opportunities within it are not evenly distributed. Where we might happen to be at that particular time, for the thing we want to do, in the way we are trying to do it, in the places we are trying to find it, there might indeed be a shortage.

However, the world is perfectly large and diverse enough to provide millions of potential opportunities in how, where, and with what we live our lives. It's just not distributing them fairly, so if we want one, we can't expect it to come and find us. We have to go to where those opportunities are being given out, and we have to jump up and down in front of them and shout, "Me, me, me!"

It's my turn.

If opportunities are not abundant where we are, we have to go where they are. If we want a beautiful spouse, we should move to Scandinavia, or Israel, or Argentina, or wherever it is that our definition of beautiful is in abundance. The odds of us acquiring a beautiful spouse will increase greatly when everyone we see and talk to is beautiful. I believe they call that math. If we want a job, in just the same way, we need to position ourselves where the unemployment rate is very low—like in a country with a booming economy—rather than waiting out our time in one languishing in a recession. Somewhere our skills are greatly in demand. Or we can learn a skill high in demand, like Web development or electrical engineering.

There's no point locating ourselves where there's scarcity, then complaining that opportunities are scarce. It makes no sense to earn minimum wage living in London, Munich, or New York when we can earn minimum wage and see it go far farther by living in Leicester, Magdeburg, or New Jersey.

If we want to learn Spanish, we can move to rural Spain for half a year, where we'll be forced to learn it. The fastest way to fall in love? Again, play the odds. If we go meet a hundred members of our desired sex, there's a very, very good chance we'll fall in love with one them. While our English Lit degree might not be of much use in Oldenburg, Oldham, or Omaha, it might come in handy in Okinawa, Japan, where we could earn a nice wage teaching the locals English.

I know this is an uncomfortable truth for many of us, and I wish it were not so. If we want opportunities in the digital age, we have to *busk*. The opportunities are going go via the back door, not the front. So we have to enlarge our networks, go to every Meetup and networking event we can, and make an impression. Be our own disciples. Our own Bible salesmen. Our own evangelists. Showcase our skills. Just last week I was at a tech Meetup here in Berlin, and a programmer was walking around with an "I'M THE EMPLOYEE YOU ARE LOOKING FOR" t-shirt and matching business cards. I probably talked to 20 different people that night. He's the only one I still remember. I'm sure he's employed by now, for all of these reasons.

Humans have been migrating for work or better opportunities since the first ape climbed down from the trees. Of course, there is a lot consider—visas, family, friends, language, culture. But it's certainly possible, and only getting easier because of the prevalence of English, social networks like Couchsurfing or Meetup.com, and just being able to Skype home whenever we like.

I don't want to make it sound flippantly easy. I know a lot of people don't have the self-confidence to raise their heads above life's pulpit and say "pick me!" It's inconvenient that they should have to. But then it's also inconvenient to be unemployed. Inconvenient to be badly paid. Inconvenient to live in a really expensive city that takes 70% of your income just in rent. Inconvenient to be bald. Inconvenient to be a plastic whistle seller. Inconvenient to have to shovel cement in winter. Inconvenient that no one is coming to pick us. Inconvenient that we might have to leave a place that we love, or friendships that we value. But, at some point, the inconvenience of inaction, passivity, or unfairness is greater than the fear of failure, of action, of inconvenience, of having to make that first positive step.

Opportunity is Darwinian. It doesn't go to the smartest or strongest, but to the most flexible. *We need to be the most flexible.*

Enlarge Your Luck Surface Area

An easy framework for putting all these complementary ideas together is that of the *Luck Surface Area*. It's a concept coined by entrepreneur, Jason Roberts: "When you pour energy into a passion, you develop an expertise, and an expertise of any kind is valuable. But quite often that value can actually be magnified by the number of people who are made aware of it. The reason is that when people become aware of your expertise, some percentage of them will take action to capture that value, but quite often it will be in a way you would never have predicted. Maybe they'll want to hire you, or partner with you, or invest in you...it will be serendipitous.[62]"

Expressed mathematically, our Luck Surface Area is:

Talent (thing we are good at) x *Number of people who know about it*

Every person has their own Luck Surface Area. It's like a big net that we carry around behind us for catching opportunities. Whether those opportunities take the form of new friendships, lovers, high-paying projects, business opportunities, lucrative job offers, TV interviews, book deals, or all expense paid trips to Jamaica, we just can't know in advance.

Simply put, the bigger we make our Luck Surface Area through a) developing an expertise and b) networking/marketing/busking that expertise, the more opportunities that will get caught within it. Consequently, the more choices we will then have to pick from.

Now, remember all that we've covered in the past few chapters:

1. The world is not fair.

2. You can't control *what* opportunities you get.
- There are simply too many unknowns. We don't know who is waiting around the corner, or who we'll end up randomly sitting next to on a plane, or that the guy at the end of the bar is looking for someone with our exact skill set.

3. But, we can control *the number* of opportunities that come our way.
- We can do this by increasing the size of our Luck Surface Area. We increase it by marketing ourselves more. By boarding that plane. By starting a conversation with that guy at the end of the bar. By increasing the size of our network. The more flexible we are about what we do and where we are willing to do it, the more we focus on following a system instead of chasing a prescribed goal, the bigger our net becomes, and the more opportunities we will catch within it.

Typically, people focus mostly on improving their skill. But they are far less comfortable busking with it. I have programmer friends who've spent years building these beautiful, technical solutions to some small problem or another. Their talent is unquestionable, their commitment obvious. However, when it comes time to launch, they devote about 0.1% of the time they invested in building their solution to telling the world about it through marketing.

It's as if, because they've built the best solution, it is just going to magically be found and appreciated—as if the world were fair.

Marketing? *Ugh.*

Marketing is uncomfortable. It's not their skill area. They would have to talk to people. They would be afraid of inconveniencing them. As a result, their Luck Surface Area and the Luck Surface Area of their project stays very small. Their perfect little Taj Mahal exists, but they've spent no time putting out any sign posts pointing people to it, so, logically, few people ever find it.

Marketing is how we recalibrate the broken machine that is life—to get attention for our talents, to increase our Luck Surface Area, to get the opportunities we deserve. It's hammering those "TAJ MAHAL THIS WAY --->" "TAJ MAHAL 200M" "NEARLY THERE" "KEEP GOING!" signs into the ground.

The universe has more than enough opportunity for us, but you have to increase the odds that it can find you by enlarging your Luck Surface Area. Everything we've learnt so far in this book is building towards that aim. The Internet and its ability to remove gatekeepers is making the process easier than ever.

Whether it's changing where you live (placing yourself in an area of abundance, or somewhere your skills are in demand), how you live (using the Freedom Figure to minimise your costs to keep you in the game long enough to get your lucky break), or how you work (creating a system that allows you to plug slowly away without always feeling like a failure for not meeting a prescribed goal), if you apply these techniques, you will find yourself, one day, at the front of the opportunity queue saying, "Today really was the day..."

"Inside every cynical person, there is a disappointed idealist." –
George Carlin

"That's one of the remarkable things about life. It's never so bad
that it can't get worse." – Bill Watterson, creator of Calvin & Hobbs

Chapter 13 - IF r > g, THEN Self-Employment > Employment

In 2014, there was a very unlikely worldwide bestseller in the form of a rather dry, 700-page doorstop written by a largely unknown French economist called Thomas Piketty. It was entitled *Capital in the 21st Century*. Normally, 700-page books written by economists, full of sentences like "The inheritance law that derived from the French Revolution and the Civil Code that followed rested on two main pillars: the abolition of substitutions héréditaires and primogeniture and the adoption of the principle of equal division of property among brothers and sisters (equipartition)," do not ordinarily become bestsellers. So, why was *Capital in the 21st Century* so warmly embraced by the zeitgeist?

An old English teacher told me that the job of all great literature is to "guide the reader to what they always suspected, but couldn't put into words." I think this is why *Capital in the 21st Century* became such a hit. It put into words what many people had long suspected. Admittedly, it did so through many, many words, graphs, and statistics. Perhaps more than some would have liked. But *put* it did.

What was it that people had long suspected? That financial inequality is increasing within the developed world. That inequality, while a natural part of the capitalist system, is now out of control. The game is rigged by design. Not only are the rich getting richer and the poor are getting poorer, but all at an accelerating rate.

This was controversial because many policy makers (and society's wealthy) have long assured us that wealth trickles down, from them to the masses, via the free market. All we have to do is leave them alone and not bother them with pesky things like regulation. They'll invest their capital in the sort of businesses that create the sort of jobs that will create the wages that we can turn into our own capital. Then, finally, it will allow us to become them. But Pikkety showed (at least in the eyes of his converts) that rather than wealth trickling down, it flows up. *Then just sits there.*

There's a simple equation at the heart of the book (well, simple by the lofty standards of the rest of the book), which Pikkety himself says represents "the fundamental force for divergence" and "sums up the overall logic of my conclusions.[63]"

That equation is: $r > g$

r = the average rate of return on capital (how much existing wealth is increasing in value).

g = the economic growth rate (how fast the economy is increasing in value).

If the economy is growing quickly, existing capital is less important, because everyone is getting wealthier and accumulating wealth that can become capital.

If the economy is growing slowly, however, there are less opportunities for people without wealth to acquire it. The people that already have it also have less of an incentive to invest it. They can leave their money in safe investments, like government bonds or a savings account offering a few percent interest, and still out-perform the economy. In this kind of scenario, wealth doesn't flow down from rich to poor. Those that have capital sit back, relax, and live from their capital without having to labour further. Meanwhile, people like us, who rely on our labour to provide us a paycheck, will always need to keep labouring away, year after year, and will still struggle to acquire capital.

Broadly speaking, when r is greater than g, society has a problem.

Pikkety concluded that there was a period, in fact, where we didn't have a problem, and r was less than g. This was the time from the end of the First World War right up until the hyper, technology fueled push towards globalisation that began in the 1970s and '80s. But he argues that this was rather unique in human history. "There was also an exceptionally high growth rate. That was partly due to the recovery from the war, but also partly due to the demographic transition. There was a Baby Boom in the mid 20th century that was unusually large," he said.

Since then, we've defaulted back to $r > g$. "Pretty much everywhere, including in the US, what you see is that the top of the wealth distribution is rising two, three times as fast as the average wealth, and as the size of the economy.[64]"

The returns for owners of capital are greater than the returns for the people labouring for that capital, which probably explains why only only one in five Germans believes economic conditions in Germany are "fair," and almost 90% feel that the gap between rich and poor is "getting wider and wider.[65]"

The main conclusion of *Capital in the 21st Century* is that we should change the way we regulate the economy, from taxing capital and labour to taxing wealth. Pikkety's suggestion is that we do this with a progressive annual tax. So, rather than just paying tax on the income from your job, you would pay tax instead on the assets you've acquired with that income—dividends from your shares, rental income from property, the savings in your bank account. Despite having become a poster child for the leftwing anti-capitalism scene, Pikkety has no problem with the accumulation of wealth. He doesn't want to stop people getting rich, since the possibility of getting rich is one of the major motivational drivers powering the capitalist system. Pikkety just wants an economy in which it is easy to get rich, but very hard to stay rich. Which sounds, really, rather logical.

"The way it would work is that if you own a house worth $500,000, but you have a mortgage of $490,000, then your net wealth is

$10,000, so in my system you would owe no tax...My point is not to increase taxation of wealth. It's actually to reduce taxation of wealth for most people, but to increase it for those who already have a lot of wealth.[66]"

However logical this might sound, it would be a major legislative reform and a change that the already wealthy would spend a lot of their wealth trying to stop from happening—those same wealthy who already occupy a lot of the positions of power that could pass this kind of reform. Which only makes the odds of it occurring even smaller. It will take a major uprising or mobilised, engaged citizenship to push it through. The book is a bestseller, however, so there's a chance that it will happen, and there will be further debate about financial inequality. But I wouldn't bet my non-existent capital on it.

As someone who read the book (full disclosure: skim read) but doesn't want to rely on legislative change to ensure my future prosperity, I was left at the end of it with a different conclusion—*I have to acquire capital*. This is something I'd long suspected from years of self-employment, but that Pikkety's research really hammered home to me.

If r is greater than g, labouring away at g doesn't make sense. Completing work that doesn't scale doesn't make sense. Swapping time for money doesn't make sense. This is very much a central tenet of this book, and all the chapters that follow. As an employee, the chances of us getting rich, or even just acquiring capital, are greatly limited by physics: There is only one of us. Which is regrettable, because we are just great. By being an employee, we swap time for money. Therefore, if we want to increase our income, we have two choices: a) We can work more hours, or b) we can charge more per hour. Working more hours is not a scalable solution, because there are only 24 of them in each day, and we also have to do a whole bunch of awkward, time-consuming human things like eating, sleeping, socialising, exercising, and checking Facebook, or we'll break down.

Charging more per hour is possible, but only up to a point where our salary demands are far higher than other people willing to do our job, otherwise our pragmatic bosses will pick them instead of us. We can get around that problem by becoming more qualified. But the more we earn and the more specialised we become, the greater incentive there is for someone to acquire their own capital by inventing a new technology, whether machine, software, or some other sort of artificial intelligence to break down our specialism. Over time, the most complex parts of our job will be simplified and standardised, and the amount of money we can ask for completing them will decrease.

"…There is increasingly no such thing as a high-wage, middle-skilled job—the thing that sustained the middle class in the last generation…Every middle-class job today is being pulled up, out or down faster than ever," says Thomas L. Friedman, journalist for the *New York Times*. "My generation had it easy. We got to 'find' a job. But, more than ever, our kids will have to 'invent' a job.[67]"

In a time of abundance, when job security is high and r is less than g, it would make more sense to be an employee and swap our talents for a reliable wage. If we are paid well and enjoy our work, there's nothing wrong with that arrangement. When done right, it is mutually beneficial to both us and our employers. But what we're seeing in recent years, and discussed at length in Chapter 4, is the breakdown of the traditional employee/employer relationship: decreasing job security, increasingly temporary forms of employment, wages increasing slower than inflation, and $r > g$—altogether, a worse deal for employees.

On the other hand, the returns from being our own bosses are only increasing. Own our own businesses, however small, even if it's just a side income, and we have the chance to sell something other than time—something that does scale and allows us to accumulate wealth, which can become capital.

Many of the skills we need to find a job in the competition of today—the self-starting, self-marketing skills discussed in the last three chapters—are precisely the same skills we need to create our own businesses. If we can use them to convince clients to hire us full-time, we can also package those same skills into products or services that we sell again and again to many such clients.

I know the idea of being our your boss is alien to a lot of people, but it's actually never been easier, never required less capital, never been less risky, and never been more realistic for people to earn some or all of their income independently. We're already being forced to learn the mindset and become entrepreneurial. We can start small. We can start alongside our day jobs, even. In the Appendix I have many case studies from people who did just that.

"Opportunities are usually disguised as hard work, so most people don't recognize them." – Ann Landers

Chapter 14 - Becoming Your Own Boss

From the outside, how exactly businesses work can seem strange, appearing like some special combination of theft, magic, and evil. But from what I've seen, it's actually incredibly simple, both on and offline.

Businesses just solve problems. For money. *Repeatedly.*

By way of an example, I'm writing this from Tel Aviv, Israel, where I'm on a month-long holiday. As I sat in the plane that delivered me to this exotic, foreign shoreline, I was not worried that I had no idea how to get from Tel Aviv airport to my accommodation in the city center (as per usual, I'd done zero research). I was not worried because I knew other people—millions of them, in fact—would have already had this exact problem. Thousands of people land at Tel Aviv airport every day, and if they're as badly organised as me, they have no idea how to reach the city center.

Because of this, there is money to be made by any business that offers to solve this problem for us. Presumably, they will do that with wheels. Sure enough, when I arrived, I found there was a mix of bus companies, train companies, car rental companies, and taxi companies, all happy to tax me for my ignorance and bad planning with their wheel-shaped solutions. I decided to take a taxi, which charged a little more than the bus, but got me there faster. This was (most likely, I didn't ask) driven by a self-employed person operating his own little business of one, solving people's logistics problems, one fare at a time.

That taxi dropped me at a room I'd rented via a service called Airbnb. Airbnb allows you to rent people's spare rooms, or even their whole apartments, while they are away. Airbnb exists to solve two problems:

1. Hotels are usually expensive, sterile, and boring.

2. People sometimes have spare rooms or spare houses, which they have to pay for even if they're not in them.

Airbnb connects the two, and allowed me to rent a room from a man called Shmulik who has a spare bedroom in his pleasant two-room apartment. Our transaction was mutually beneficial, but it would have been almost impossible, or at least highly impractical, without the Airbnb service to connect us both. Now Shmulik makes a little money from his empty bedroom, I save a little money while making a friend, and Airbnb earns a cut by solving both our problems.

This very morning, my first in the city, I woke up hungry. The café around the corner knows that enough people get hungry each morning that it makes sense to put on the breakfast special that enticed me to not breakfast at home (well, Shmulik's home). Later in the day I got tired and couldn't write any more of these words. No problem, because of *caffeine*. The Coca-Cola Company produces a curious brown caffeinated sludge on an industrial scale, stuffed with the near legal limit of servable sugar and caffeine. They've done a truly remarkable job of distributing this to almost every possible corner of the earth where sugar junkies and caffeine addicts might hope to find it. Coke might not be the best product, but it certainly has the best distribution. It's officially available in all but two countries in the world (Cuba and North Korea), and allegedly "Coke" is the second most known word in the world, after "ok." It solved my caffeine and sugar problem, as it says it does more than 1.4 billion times every day, all around the world.

Simple so far, right? *Find problem, sell solution.*

With an online business, the *how* might be different, since the Internet offers certain advantages like being able to sell to the whole world from day one, or being able to sell something digital. But the *what* doesn't change. You still have to find a problem and solve it. You have to sell that solution for less than the cost of providing it, and you have to repeat this individual transaction again and again.

That's it.

Not All Businesses Are Equal

Of course, all businesses are different. Some are big, like McDonalds. Some are small, like the little Italian man who owns the cafe across from my house, which only seems to be open about an hour a day and I think is possibly a mob front. Some are highly profitable, like Coca-Cola, and possibly mobstering (although that's for different reasons). Others have high revenues but low profits, like Amazon. Some sell thousands of different types of products, like my local supermarket. Some sell just one type, like the publisher of this book.

If you're thinking of starting your own business—and I believe it makes more and more sense to consider that—then you first have to find a problem and solve it, and, ideally, solve it in a way that scales.

When some businesses grow, so does the amount of money they make—but equally, so does the amount of work they must do. When scalable businesses grow, however, so does the amount of money they make, but (at least proportionally) the amount of work they do does not. In order to maximise the time where you can be practicing Beatles songs on the guitar, or chasing a butterfly in a field, or building that island, it's easy to see which one of the two is preferable.

Broadly speaking, and allowing for massive simplification, it's the difference between a *service business* (which involves doing something over and over again for every new customer) like a traditional letting agent, a psychologist, a lawyer, or a dentist, and a *product business* (which involves doing something once then selling it over and over with minimal differences).

The taxi driver is a good example. Unless something has gone very wrong with the laws of physics, he can only be in one place at one time. If he wants to make twice as much money, he needs to double all of his costs—a second car, a second him, twice as much petrol. *His business does not scale.*

The great thing about the digital revolution is that online businesses have the potential to scale fantastically well. Here's an example from my own very miniature digital empire: Last night, in Schmulik's spare bed, I went to sleep. Not exactly original, I know—I've actually done that several times before. You probably have too. What was different about my sleep, compared to the sleep of employed people, is that, when I woke up, I was richer. Of course, due to my limited skill set and the mediocrity of my offerings, in the eight hours I was sleeping, I probably only became about €20 richer from my Internet businesses and books. But that's still a very profitable sleep, and it's pretty much my fault I didn't make more. Better products + better marketing = more profitable sleeps and more profitable days.

What's important and fundamental and special is that it is realistic for us, if we so choose, to build businesses where we work just once and yet get paid multiple times, passively, without being there. *Passive income*. Once you've experienced it, it's like a little light bulb pings on, and for the first time you're out of the dark and you go, "That just makes sense." But they don't teach this stuff where they should, which is everywhere, all the time.

I learnt the hard way the difference between a good Internet business (a passive, scalable one) and a bad Internet business (active, non-scalable), because I've started one of each.

My Route to Self-Employment – TheTeeDirectory

In 2008, I'd just finished working for an ecommerce apparel startup in Germany called Spreadshirt. Spreadshirt is an online platform where anyone can upload a design they have made and offer it for sale on several dozen different products, the most popular of which is a t-shirt. I worked there as an Internet marketer, and in that year I learnt a lot about the apparel industry. I saw that while there were many excellent designers using the Spreadshirt platform to create great looking products, they didn't usually have the marketing skills to sell them. Spreadshirt had several hundred thousand shop partners, and there were at least 10 competitors to Spreadshirt who had similarly sized armies of designers creating products.

In total, that's millions of small online t-shirt brands with great products, struggling to find customers for them. I decided I'd try and solve this problem in a simple way, by creating a central database for t-shirt brands. Customers would be able to search for specific t-shirts, read reviews from previous customers, and find out about special offers and coupons for their companies. I'd charge them to be promoted in my search engine. I also knew many of these brands had their own affiliate programs. These programs track when you send the company a customer, and pay you a small fee for it—usually 10–20% of whatever the customer spends.

I called my proposed website TheTeeDirectory, short for The T-shirt Directory.

Since I can neither program nor design, I knew I wouldn't be able to build this website on my own. I didn't have the technical skills. But similar review and directory sites existed for different products and services, so there were plenty of examples of the type of search and gallery functions I wanted to have on my site that I could copy.

So, I prepared a detailed process document of how the site should look and function. Every page was documented in the form of simple mockups created in Microsoft Word, using the drawing tool and lots of annotated square text boxes. It looked, well, truly awful. Since I was travelling at the time, I decided to hire a remote worker from the USA to build the site, the advantage being that we'd share a language, making communication easy. The dollar was also pretty weak against the euro at the time, so the cost would be cheaper than finding someone locally once I was back in Europe.

I created a job ad on a remote worker platform called Upwork. Over the years, I've used Upwork to hire dozens of remote employees for my businesses. There, you can find almost anyone to perform remote tasks for you—like programming, graphic design, accountancy, content creation, or personal assistants. You decide what you want, and remote workers around the world bid for the project, as many did for mine. I had bids from $250 to $2500. I hired one that had good reviews and that asked a fixed, fair price (not the cheapest, but also not the most expensive). It turned out to be a small digital agency of one designer and two programmers, based in Baltimore, USA. I agreed to pay them in three instalments—a third upfront, a third after they completed the design, and a third after they built the website.

I sent them my process document and we began to spec the site together. We agreed the site would be based on Wordpress (the most popular website/blog administration tool), albeit in a heavily customised form, since I wanted functions Wordpress didn't offer. We never met in person. Never talked via the phone or Skyped. Just emailed back and forth, and then, a month later, after working with my process document, they sent me the first design drafts of the pages that would make of the site. It was completely unrecognisable from my early boxy plans, and this was a good thing. They'd created something really outstanding, adding so many ideas and improvements to my early plans that it was almost a completely new website. We did a final round of consultation and changes. Another month later they presented me with the finished solution. In total, I paid them a little over €1250 for it.

Next, I had to fill it with content. Some of this was automated, but the vast majority was not. So I started filling the directory by hand. Once I had a good idea how to add content quickly, I created another very ugly Microsoft Word process guide and hired three remote workers via Upwork to help me fill it up. It took about three months, at least a 150 hours of my own time, and another €400 before I could launch the site, and by then it had more than 500 t-shirt brands featured, reviewed, and available for search. At least 50 of those offered affiliate programs. This was how the site made money. People came from Google for search terms related to t-shirts, such as "spiderman t-shirt usa" or "skater clothing Germany." They found my site, browsed around, clicked some affiliate links, and went off and bought some t-shirts.

The website was profitable within six months. I eventually kept one of those remote workers on—a student named Ivy—and she ended up running the site for me for the next three years. I would log in occasionally and check everything was okay, and try to optimise certain pages to rank higher in Google. By the end of the first year I was earning about €1500 a month in profit. I had exceeded my Freedom Figure, and I was only investing a few hours a week. Ivy continued working, I continued marketing, and by the end of year two the site was generating a profit of around €3000 a month. It remained my primary income for about three and a half years, the last two of which I didn't work at all. I didn't even log in. Ivy kept the site going, working around 10 hours a week for about €10 an hour. My original developers and design team would occasional add new features or fix up bugs on a per hour basis (around €40 an hour, from memory, but since they built the site they knew how it worked and so could quickly make changes). It was, in many ways, the perfect business. It solved a problem. But more than that, it scaled beautifully, as we only offered information. Just text on a page.

Not only was the business truly scalable, but I could also run it from anywhere. All I needed was my laptop and an Internet connection. I spent a lot of those early years travelling and thinking how lucky I was, and wondering why more people weren't trying to build a business like this. A *passive income business.*

My Route to Self-Employment Part 2 – The Hipstery

About a year and a half after I started TheTeeDirectory, once it was already providing more than my monthly Freedom Figure, I decided to forget everything I'd learnt—all the reasons why it was such a fantastic business—and instead build a not very good second business that was its complete opposite. I called it *The Hipstery.*

I knew from my time at Spreadshirt and from running TheTeeDirectory that many of these small t-shirt companies were producing products that they simply couldn't sell. These products would grow dusty in the corners of warehouses, blocking money that the businesses could be using to create products that did sell.

Just as TheTeeDirectory was helping them market their businesses, I decided I'd build a new business that would help them shift some the over-stock that they couldn't sell. The Hipstery would be a mystery product experience. People would visit the website and answer a funny, six-question survey about themselves. Afterwards, they'd be invited to buy a mystery t-shirt from us that we promised them would be matched perfectly to their tastes, as determined from their survey answers. We would pick the most fitting t-shirt for them, ship it to them, and it would be a mystery until the second they opened it.

Some businesses scale; others do not. *The Hipstery did not.*

The TeeDirectory offered an all-digital good—*information*. Whether this sentence is read by no one, only my mum (hiya!), or a million people, I only have to write it once. If the TheTeeDirectory was viewed by 10 people per day or 100 people a day—or if we received a big write-up from a well-trafficked blog and 10,000 people came in one day—how much extra work had to be done? Pretty much none. Maybe we'd get a few more emails to answer, but that was it.

The Hipstery offered physical goods—*t-shirts*. On a normal day, at first, we might only have five orders. So we had to pick five t-shirts, fold five t-shirts, prepare five receipts, pack five orders, and post five orders, all of which took time and required someone's physical presence. Obviously, I was buying over-stock t-shirts in advance, but that had its own problems, as the supply was not always reliable. Also, I had to invest money up front in t-shirts, without knowing how popular they might be. Secondly, since I was selling t-shirts in multiple sizes, I had to stock t-shirts across eight different sizes (S to XL) and two different genders. So I had to estimate demand for those genders and sizes in advance.

Now what do you think happened on those days when we were featured in the press and, instead of getting five orders, we would get 250 orders? Chaos would happen, that's what.

Because we had a direct link to the customers, we had customer service to do. With TheTeeDirectory we had no direct link to our customers. We were just pushing traffic around. We were middlemen. We didn't sell anything. We didn't have to ship anything. We didn't have to do customer service or after-sales care. With the Hipstery, I had to do all of those things. Days with 250 orders meant packing 250 t-shirts (which we usually ran out of and so had to scramble to find more, or print them ourselves). Folding 250 t-shirts. Preparing 250 receipts, packing 250 orders, stamping and carrying 250 orders to the post office. Providing customer service for 250 orders. Replacing those lost in the post. Processing returns from customers who didn't like their mystery t-shirts.

The Hipstery was a vastly cooler business, and loved by its small, loyal customer base, but it never managed to pay me or generate a significant profit. It did, however, do a fantastic job of monopolizing nearly all my time, and causing me the sort of daily stress that probably resulted in my going bald. A few years later, I closed it down. In comparison, The Tee Directory just kept on making money and being, well, pretty much the perfect business.

You can see TheTeeDirectory vs The Hipstery playing out again and again. Guitar teachers can give one-on-one or group lessons, but that business, like The Hipstery, can't scale very easily because they only have two arms. They might be self-employed, but they're still swapping their time for money, like an employee does. However, if they so chose, they could also video record the lessons they give, then make a whole series of those lessons and sell them online instead as a "learn guitar" course on a service like Sofatutor or Udemy. Then they're getting closer to TheTeeDirectory, by selling something digital and passive. In the same way, stand-up comedians can become YouTube channel owners, yoga teachers can turn into yoga mat manufacturers, travel brokers can turn into flight search engines, flea markets can become eBay, craft fairs can become craft marketplaces like Etsy, newspaper classifieds can become online white pages like Craigslist, record stores can become Spotify, real estate brokers can become Immoscout, holiday apartment brokers can become Airbnb, and people who work hard can become people who take a lot more naps.

Create, sell repeatedly, outsource.

It's a slow push from analogue to digital, from services to products (since products are standardised, they are easier to sell passively), from bundled services (like cable TV packages) to streamlined products (like Netflix), from non-scalable to high-scale, disruptive, centralised marketplaces.

There is no such thing as a zero effort, high reward business. It's a myth. "There is no such thing as set-it-and-forget-it online content-driven revenue," says Pamela Slim, author of *Escape from Cubicle Nation*. That said, some businesses are created from the outset with passivity as a goal, and that goal informs all the decision about how they are structured. "It takes time, effort, and energy to maintain interest in the product...and this takes marketing effort that is not 'passive,'" she warns.

Of course, despite my best intentions and blatant propaganda, not everyone will want to go the self-employed route, even if it is just to dabble with an Internet side project. That's fine. In the words of Escape Cubicle Nation's Pamela Slim, "Your day-to-day happiness doesn't have much to do with your form of employment. Working for yourself will not magically make all your problems go away and lift your mood."

There's also definitely something to be said for being a regular nine-to-five employee—for finding an employer, aligning your goals and expectations, and then making a commitment to each other. Plus, you have a contract between you and your employer that dictates that at x date of every month, x amount of money will be transferred to your bank account. They can cancel that, but only under certain circumstances, and they have to give you a certain amount of warning first. This buys you some financial certainty. This kind of financial certainty is a big plus if you want to take out any kind of large financial debt such as a mortgage.

In the long term, however, I think the idea that full-time employment is safer than self-employment is a bit of a fallacy. Maybe in the past it was the case, or it's true in certain public sector industries, but for all the reasons already discussed in this book—the speed of change within markets, encroaching automation, over-supply of workers—loyalty between employer and employee has eroded to the point where it can no longer be reasonably expected in the private sector. Nature gives us two eyes and two legs and two kidneys for a reason, and that reason is not because it's a fan of symmetry. Redundancy rules. If you are completely reliant on one company to provide for you, all your eggs are in one financial basket, and that's a vulnerable situation. Employment legislation is on your side, but there are many options open to a company if they decide they want you out.

Recently, a friend here in Berlin passed her six-month assessment at a new job, and thought that, since it would be nearly impossible for an employer to fire her, and since they let her pass her probation period where they also gave her an excellent review, she must be doing a good job. Six weeks later she was called into the office and told that a major customer contract had been cancelled, and she was being let go. Whether that contract was really cancelled is hard to know. The company reported that they were not financially able to keep the person on, and even though she had an unlimited contract, she was let go. If an employer wants you out, for whatever reason, there are many ways they can do it. At another company I worked for, they searched the Internet browsing history of an employee they wanted to fire but had no grounds to, found a website he'd viewed that violated the IT policy he'd signed when hired, and used this as grounds for his dismissal. Earlier in the book I told the story of the people on my integrations course who were replaced by several mini-jobbers after the minimum wage increased. It's not that being an employee is less safe—it's just not a safe as people often make it sound. You're like an investor who bets the house on just one stock each month.

If you decide self-employment is not right for you, and prefer to be an employee or a freelancer, you still have important work to do to prosper in the digital age, in the face of high uncertainty, rapid change, and increasing automation. We'll look now at each in turn.

Excelling As an Employee in the Digital Age

While remaining committed to your employer, it makes sense to always be keeping your skills up to date, your eye on the developments in the job market, and your network growing within your industry. My driving instructor used to have a mantra he repeated every time we approached a roundabout, which I think is relevant here: "Be ready to go, but prepared to stay."

1. Make contingency plans.

Many businesses have contingency plans, such as what happens if their biggest supplier goes bust, or a plane flies into their silo. These plans dictate how they will react so that they don't need to plan if the worst happens, and they have a better chance of reacting rationally and calmly to the new situation. It makes just as much sense for us, as employees, to have the same. What if I get given a new boss that I can't work with? What if the firm goes bust? What if my job is made obsolete? What if there is a round of layoffs in my department? How many months of my Freedom Figure do I have in my savings account? If I were to be laid off, how could I quickly downgrade my lifestyle? Understanding how you would react in that situation—regardless of whether it is how you actually react—can already begin to lessen the stress and anxiety. The unimaginable becomes imaginable, and you have time to mentally prepare.

2. Always be learning.

It's your duty to keep your skills up to date. Fortunately, this is easier than ever because of all the distance learning portals like *Udemy* and *Sofatutor,* where you can study in your free time. Develop new skills before you need them. Look to build skills that are complementary to those you already have, that overlap well with your core skills, and which will be hard to automate.

There's plenty of debate over whether one main specialism or several generalisms is the best protection for future employees. "We've become a society that's data rich and meaning poor," believes author Carter Phipps. Specialists have their place. However, "there are truths that can only be revealed by a generalist who can weave these ideas in the broader fabric of understanding.[68]"

In the smaller and leaner organizations of today, specialism does not always mean safety for employees. Smaller companies are solving smaller problems with smaller numbers of staff. When they look outside of the company, it might be just to fill one specific function that they need now, but not often enough to hire someone full-time. Lawyers are a good example of this. Because of the complexity, risk, and specialism involved in their job, lawyers command a high salary. As a result, only mid-sized to large companies would consider having one on their full-time staff. The rest of us hire a lawyer when we need them, and pay per hour. Now, more and more of us are, whether through choice or necessity, being employed in just the same kind of way. We're slowly becoming lawyers. If you want to stay a nine-to-five employee, and if you have too high of specialism that isn't part of a company's core competency, you might just end up like the lawyer—too expensive to have on staff, too specialised to be needed full-time. To avoid this, a mix of skills is desirable. "The future will be about becoming and being masterful. It's a combination of knowing something deeply and becoming skilled in a variety of competencies," says Lynda Gratton, author of *The Shift: The future of work is already here*. "Value in the future will come through being able to combine different areas of depth to create value," she believes. So the programmer who can also design and has experience with online marketing, the sales person who can also write copy, or the HR person who is also a whizz at Excel and knows enough about the firm's intranet system to manage the department's intranet site will be better appreciated. Overlapping a deep specialism with several related generalisms or experience in different sectors and industries is a good idea. "In today's uncertain environment, breadth of perspective trumps depth of knowledge," says *Harvard Business Review*'s Vikram Mansharamani.[69]

3. Read the writing on the wall.

While it's often hard to forecast exactly what is going to happen in your industry, roughly speaking, you can follow the curve of automation in your area and work out when it will affect your job. You can witness this happening today in journalism. Journalism is still relevant. Journalism is still important. People still want to read news and opinions. It's just that the Internet is destroying the economics of their delivery. As a result, there are less full-time salaried jobs for journalists, as a mass amateurisation is occurring. The future of publishing is likely to follow a similar trajectory. Ebooks don't have to make the the printed book obsolete, they just have to undermine its economics enough that the businesses that support it—the bookstores, publishers, printers, agents, and distributors—collapse away.

If you're working in an industry like this, your goal is not to keep doing your job until it's no longer needed, but to evolve new skills that keep you ahead of that curve of automation. You should be developing new skills before you actually need them; to always be the one in the company that people look to to explain new developments and technologies occurring within the industry. Change always happens far slower than people like me—who are interested in the future—imagine. There's little change for a long time, then suddenly a tipping point is reached, and markets appear to collapse and be rebuilt anew almost overnight.

4. Network before you need your network.

Networking is an essential part of finding opportunities in the digital age. As already discussed, taking time to network and increasing your *Luck Surface Area* is the best way to advance your career. If you're public facing in your position, you can try and use social media to build a following on a neutral site like Xing, Linkedin, Facebook, Twitter, or a personal blog. The goal is to present yourself as an industry expert in whatever you do. If you then decide to change jobs or find yourself without work, you can use the network you've built to find a new position. Since you've already demonstrated your expertise over time and bring a certain amount of loyal online fans with you, you won't have to convince them of your worth.

5. Focus on what is hard to automate.

Managing spreadsheets and creating reports? Easy. Managing people, with their various whims and moods? Difficult. Fuzzy jobs, where the work is always different, where the clients change, where you offer a bespoke service—these should be safer spots. High-skill and low-routine is where you want to be if you want the best chance of avoiding the robots.

6. Negotiate time out of the office.

While being an employee might offer less freedom than freelancing or self-employment, long gone are the days when you need be chained to your desk. Try and negotiate home office with your company at least one day a week. Many companies are pretty backward when it comes to the idea of letting their employees work remotely, which is why it is important to start small and convince them it is also to their benefit. If you can just negotiate an occasional day from home—and they see that you are still available, still sending emails, still being as productive—you can slowly nudge them towards further off-site days. Having time out of the office will help you clear important tasks and work on more speculative projects without distractions, reminding the company just how useful you are when you're not bogged down in an endless cycle of meetings.

Freelancing in the Digital Age

When I worked at Microsoft, we had two classes of employee—FTEs (full-time employees) and freelancers. FTEs—permanent staff members—were the top of the hierarchy. We officially worked for Microsoft, could attend the company parties, had a Microsoft pension, got discount stock and products, and enjoyed all the other perks that came with working for a company previously voted the best employer in the UK. Beneath us permanent employees was a small army of freelance workers employed by staffing agencies like Manpower or Brook Street. These people did the same jobs as the permanent staff, but received very few of Microsoft employee benefits. They could not attend Microsoft company parties, buy discounted products, or have a company pension.

Employing freelancers instead of FTEs has several advantages for Microsoft. Firstly, they can fire these people with a much shorter notice period. Secondly, they don't have to pay for all those benefits. Thirdly, they can report a much higher EPE (earnings per employee) figure in their financial reports, since freelancer workers don't count as employees in the eyes of the stock market (since they are merely a short-term liability).

Whether it makes sense for the freelancers to accept work this way depends a lot on the freelancers' long-term goals (I know that many felt frustrated at being treated inferiorly) and what they did with the approximately 50% higher wages they could command. There had been lawsuits from freelancers who were employed this way for years but denied the chance to become full-time employees. Some people liked the flexibility and extra money it offered, while others resented their lesser status and lack of job security.

The advantage of being a freelancer is that you can better maximise the market value of a particular skill by selling just that specific skill. You can focus on just your small cog, without having to worry about the health of the overall machine. That machine belongs to someone else.

Today, the Internet is also creating a new type of freelancer—the remote worker. These are even shorter-term freelancers hired by people or companies that they'll never meet in person. They might work for a business just once, for an hour, fixing a website bug. Or they might be employed a few hours a week, answering customer service emails or writing website copy. Or they may even work for many years. The Internet, and in particular sites like Upwork, are driving this type of ultra-flexible employment. If you've a talent, whether it's Microsoft Excel, graphic design, programming, writing, or data entry, you can create a profile and people all around the world can hire you. You risk nothing but a little time getting set up and bidding on projects. You don't need a website, business cards, an office, or investment funding to get up and running and find your first clients.

For many people working this way, this is perhaps an in-between step—a way to work while caring for young children, a way to work while travelling, or perhaps that first dedicated income stream that can support them while they build their own Internet businesses. This might be just as simple as finding a way to standardise the very service they are offering on these remote worker platforms, only in a more repeatable and scalable way.

Excelling as a Freelancer in the Digital Age

1. Maximise your in-demand years.

Over time, the market value of a skill will change. While an employee might be limited to asking for a pay rise once or twice a year, as a freelancer, in theory, you can reset your rates every time you change client. You are in a position to take the maximum amount of money for that particular skill, because you can keep taking short-term contracts, and, after each one, adjusting your wages to reflect demand in the market and your increased standing within it. But, despite this, many freelancers underprice themselves. "I was charging clients a measly rate because I was afraid I wasn't worth anything more. Raising my rate improved my business on all fronts," says Web designer Tyler Galpin.[70]

If your finances are under control, this is an excellent opportunity to save hard during peak skill years, then work less or live from your savings later while you are retraining and developing newly in-demand skills.

2. Take periods out to retrain.

For a full-time employee, it's usually no problem to learn on the job, or try and convince your employer to pay for your training, since they're making a long-term investment in your usefulness. However, as a contractor, you're paid a higher wage because of the skills you already have. It's likely the company already has plenty of generalists, so freelancers are usually used for a specific, high-value skills that the company needs at that moment but not regularly—otherwise they'd have a full-time employee look after it. You are expected to come in and be immediately productive, which means you have to work hard between jobs to ensure you stay up-to-date with the industry and have in-demand specialized skills.

Because you're a freelancer, it is also not expected that you have to account for every gap on your CV. You can use these gaps to travel or retrain.

3. Balance client projects with your own projects.

Being a freelancer can be a perfect in-between step for people aspiring to have their own businesses. Working full-time is not likely to leave enough spare hours to build a side business, but downsizing yourself to a few days a week or to freelancing might. Client work can be your financial bedrock, where you work just enough to get by, then invest the rest of your time into building your own business or your next career. I know a translator here in Berlin who is also an aspiring novelist. Each month she looks at her bank account and decides if she can afford to work on her novel or not. If she can't, she'll take the month off of writing, and instead do freelance translation work before returning back to her novel, her financial prosperity ensured for a few more months.

4. Work remotely.

If done correctly, this is a mode of work that is extremely compatible with raising a family. You can decide how many hours a day you can work, and just take enough work to fill that time. If you take work where you don't have to be physically present, you can often work at hours that suit you, around your family, and also from wherever you like. I hired an Indian programmer called Akshay, who had lived in the USA for several years, but returned to India where he could take client projects from Europe and the USA but benefit from the low cost of living on offer in India. He was earning in dollars, but living in rupees, and so had more time to spend with his family.

5. You are your network.

The Luck Surface Area is even more important when you're going to need a new opportunity at the end of every short-term work project. If you stay in a job for a longer period of time, you have the chance to build standing within your industry, but if you're hopping regularly between projects, it can be harder to demonstrate the value you've brought to them. "It is clear that these free-agent, knowledge-rich, dynamic, project-based jobs of the future are capable of being really fulfilling. However, because they are fragmented, with many different stakeholders, in a rapidly changing skill area, they are also capable of making you nearly invisible," says Gratton. This is why it's crucial that freelancers are excellent networkers, always busy growing their networks and spreading the word about their skills long before they need the next project. "The vast majority of hiring is friends and acquaintances hiring other trusted friends and acquaintances," says career coach Matt Youngquist.[71]

Conclusion

And so, we've reached the end. We say goodbye with a short fable. An experiment is created in which five monkeys are placed into a room. A banana is hung from the ceiling, above a central ladder. As soon as any monkey attempts to climb the ladder, all the monkeys are sprayed with freezing cold water from overhead jets.

The monkeys learn that if anyone touches the ladder, it means freezing cold water for everyone.

Next, the scientists remove one monkey and replace it with a new one. Naturally, this monkey heads straight for the ladder—at which point he is beaten up by the other monkeys. Why? Well, he doesn't know, but learns it's best not to touch the ladder.

The scientists continue swapping out the monkeys...until, in the end, you have five monkeys beating each other up to stop them touching a ladder, and not a single one of them knows the reason why.

I think this short but sweet fable perfectly illustrates some of how it is to be human. We're all monkeys released into a room that doesn't make sense to us, and informed by others how we should behave within it. As children, we first reach out for that ladder— whether it's getting dirty in the park, trying to wear a pirate outfit to school, eating dessert before the main course, or other smaller acts of harmless curiosity and defiance—only to be told by larger monkeys to step away; that this is not the way things work; that this particular ladder is out of bounds; that we are messing with the natural order of things.

Then we get older, our horizons broaden, our parents cease to be the all-knowing oracle monkeys they once were, and, instead, we inherit a series of new gatekeepers—teachers, peers, friends, politicians, neighbours, celebrities, bosses, colleagues, the police.

It's from all these people that we learn how the world works, what our place is within it, and what ladders we can and can't touch.

This would be just fine, if they had any real idea themselves. But often, just like the monkeys of our ladder experiment, they've no idea either. What they're telling us is out-of-date, wrong, an old wives' tale, anecdotal, or something even more malicious, something that aims to support a status quo that keeps them in their current positions and oppresses us beneath them. That something that they swear to us is a science is actually more like an art. It takes guts to admit that there is no higher power, no deeper meaning, no hidden logic, no optimum solution, no right decision, no one right way. Few people are comfortable admitting how little control they have over their lives, and many more will fight until their last breath to convince us otherwise.

Let them try.

Because of all this, it's very easy to bumble along, believing we're making the key decisions in our lives when really they're making us, or being made for us by others. We are living life by default, to borrow a phrase from author David Cain. "It is typical for the major aspects of a human life (career, friends, habits and home) to be decided by happenstance, and not consciously. The feeling of something huge being missing is probably often due to a serious mismatch between what you currently have in one of those aspects, and what is best for you in one of those aspects." Often, we're just following previous decisions—decisions that someone else made for us, or that we made at an earlier points in time, when we knew neither ourselves nor our options as clearly as we do today. So we live where we studied. We're friends with our colleagues, not because they're suited to us, but because we spend all day with them. We live in the country where we grew up, regardless of how hard that country might make living there. "Few people make a deliberate quest out of finding their perfect city or neighborhood, of seeking out truly like-minded people. Most of us live seventy or eighty years defending what we've been given, because we think it's who we are,[72]" says David.

Of course, it's always intimidating to make a major change to the structure of our lives, even if it's just a temporary one. To fight and struggle to keep things as they are, or have always been. But it needn't be that way. "The other side isn't hell and death. It's recovery. If you've built your possessions and relationships upon an unstable foundation, then there's a very good chance they'll crumble when you stop straining to keep them in place. Let them collapse anyway...Once your old world collapses, you can recover and rebuild. Now you have the chance to start fresh and do things more intelligently,[73]" says self-help author Steve Pavlina.

For the truth is, although our generation has its problems, we're still vastly more blessed than previous ones to be able to break out from nine-to-five drudgery and see, experience, travel, live abroad, start our own businesses, cultivate skills, find meaningful work, and market and educate ourselves. To work how we choose, when we want, from wherever we like. On a boat. In a park. From atop a sand dune. A kilometre from where we were born, or a thousand. Working with people we meet in person, or some distant avatars on our computer screens. And, lastly, if we so choose—to become our own bosses.

We have abundant opportunities. They're just not necessarily shaped or distributed like the opportunities of previous generations, nor given out by the gatekeepers. The world has changed, but not all of its rule makers have noticed. Probably no one is coming to pick us. But that's okay, because, if we want, we can pick ourselves. That's what this book has been about.

Of course, it's not an easy choice. It takes bravery, sacrifice, a willingness to leave our comfort zones, the confidence to turn up to each and every one of the opportunities in our lives, comfortable with our failures and realistic in our expectations. To calculate and optimise our Freedom Figures to allow us to live cheaply at times, and not have our incomes unnecessarily dictating our lifestyles. Staying in the game as long as possible, not trying to reach goals, but following a system that maximises our talents while also leaving space for the serendipity of an unfair, chaotic world to help decide where that talent will take us.

I think, while there is cause for great optimism, there is, at the same time, genuine reason for concern that advances in technology are reducing total employment, at least in the short term. And, that automation technologies will further polarise work between few high-skill, high-pay, high-tech jobs and many low-skill, low-pay, low-stability jobs. This only makes all of the advice in this book more urgent. If we're not careful, or don't take steps to create our own jobs or separate ourselves from the masses, then we'll be left scrapping in a game with worsening odds.

Yet, I'm meeting people all over the world who already understand this—who have understood it for years. Many of them are even featured in this book. These are people who are breaking with convention, opting out, downsizing, selling up, getting off the hedonic treadmill and reprogramming their lives to be leaner, more flexible, and more future-proof. They are people building the life they always wanted for themselves, one small piece at a time, until they get to say, *"Today really was my day..."*

Go reach for your ladder—even if it gets us all wet.

Thank you for reading and good luck. *

Not that we're done. You'll find real case studies from people who have created their own businesses or more temporary forms of employment in the Appendix.

Help me keep doing this

You made it all the way to the end? Fantastic. Thank you. You're a wonderful human. I'm extremely grateful you took a chance on me (there's a song in that, I think).

Want to know the hardest part of being a writer? It's not the words—it's everything that happens after the words. There are a lot of words out there. I'm just one little bald British man. I don't have a publisher supporting this book. I don't have a big marketing budget to help people find it. I can't put up posters of my face in the subway. I can't hire a blimp to circle the Super Bowl.

But I have something much more powerful and effective anyway, something publishers would kill for—**a group of loyal readers**. Readers like you. Honest reviews work like rocket fuel for books. Writing a review is the best thing you can do to both thank me and help me write more books. I want there to be more books. I hope you do too.

Thank you. I owe you.

Adam

Bonus Content – An Extract from Don't Go There

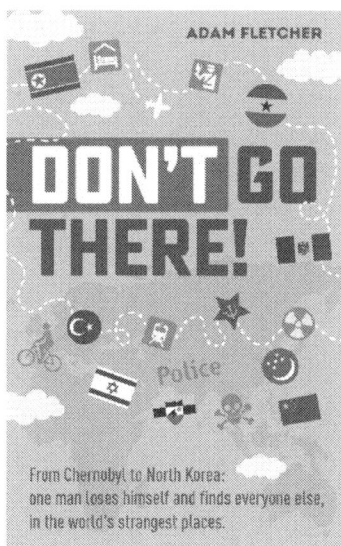

How much would you risk to change your life? *After Spiegel bestselling-author Adam Fletcher is accidentally tear-gassed in street protests in Istanbul, he goes on a journey to change his humdrum life, taking his eccentric German girlfriend, Annett, along with him. Their quest to better understand themselves (and everyone else) threatens their world view, sanity, and relationship.*

Don't Go There is a **hilarious travelogue** *full of* **interesting characters, uncomfortable moments, unusual destinations,** *and British humour that will appeal to lovers of Bill Bryson, Douglas Adams, and David Sedaris.*

It's also laughably cheap. Convinced? Great, you can get it here http://books2read.com/dont-go-there

Not convinced? Here's a nice long teaser from its Israel chapter...

I arrived at Berlin Schönefeld early, since I'd heard security can be pretty overzealous when you're heading to Israel, or are in Israel, or if you've ever been to Israel and want to go somewhere that isn't. In the departure hall, a small bearded EL AL (Israel's national airline) employee collected me at the outer ring of the system of pre-check-in counters. This was new. The man had heavy black eyebrows and thin metal glasses with circular frames.

"Good morning. My name is Levi," he said, grinning and taking my passport. Some people fit snugly into their environment—the humourless accountant, the nerdy scientist, the heavily tattooed tattoo artist. Levi was not one of these people. He was like a small Jewish cheerleader, his face permanently failing to restrain the sheer wonder that was his own existence. I found him a delightfully positive presence in the sterile, depressing, authoritarian environment of airport security. During all the weird things that were about to happen to me, that face always said, "I'm totally on your side, buddy" (no matter how firmly the rest of his body said, "YOU SHALL NOT PASS!").

"Now, Adam," he began. "Israel, is, err, as you may know..." His eyes darted diagonally upwards in search of suitably delicate wording. His tone was that of a teacher explaining basic arithmetic to the class idiot. "We're, *well*, a little bit *special*. So there will be some extra questions today. But if there are no problems, then you can proceed to the check-in counter. Okay?" He gestured to the counter over his left shoulder. A bored-looking woman sat there, waiting for someone to correctly answer enough questions to win her audience.

"Sure, no problem," I said, because I had both no choice and nothing to hide. As for Israel being special, I already knew that; it was why I was going there. Many of my friends had raved about Israel, which promised trash-free beaches, great food, interesting people, and intensity.

"Why are you flying from Germany and not from England?" Levi asked.

"Because I live here in Berlin."

"How long have you lived here in Berlin?"

"Three years, I think."

"You think?"

I cleared my throat. "Three years."

Levi's eye twinkled. "You know, you look a little bit Israeli?"

I didn't know what to say to this because I didn't really know what the average Israeli looked like. I'd only ever met one. Levi flicked through my stamps. He lingered on the ones I'd collected from Muslim countries that Israel doesn't like. Which is all of them.

"Thank you, Adam. Please just wait here a second. I'll return shortly."

I relaxed. It was over and I could now enjoy an interesting holiday. Levi approached a scary-looking man standing to the side of the check-in counter. This man had the appearance of a nightclub bouncer. He was wearing an earpiece, the cord of which disappeared into his tight blue EL AL shirt. The shirt looked stressed in its attempts to retain all of the man's muscles. He had at least three times as many as I did and had successfully exercised all of them to tautness. He didn't have a face like thunder—he had a face that seemed able to produce thunder, amongst other bad weather, all of which could be unleashed upon you at his discretion.

Levi approached him warily, like Oliver Twist asking for more gruel. The buff man eyed me like a lion might a badly wounded gazelle. The two exchanged words, and the man shook his head, slowly, keeping it perfectly level. Levi returned, smiling, as if absolutely everything was perfect and this was, in many ways, the best day of his life.

"Fantastic. Thank you for waiting," he said, as if I'd had a choice. "I'm going to need to ask you a few more questions today. Is that okay?" My shoulders slumped forward. "Can you tell me what your occupation is, Adam?"

This was a difficult question. I prided myself on my ability to function as a human without anything resembling an occupation. You may have heard of the concept of a Renaissance man. Well, I'm a pre-Renaissance man, stubbornly devoid of any skills. Technically, I could have said "journalist" or "writer." However, admitting to these professions is like uttering a special secret password to Travel Hell. No one wants journalists or writers in their country because they have a habit of writing things, and sometimes these things are even true.

"I'm a small business owner," I said. "I have a few different websites." Which was true and paid the bills better than any of my flirtations with the written word.

"What do these websites do?"

"I have one called The Hipstery, where I sell products, and one called TheTeeDirectory where I recommend them."

He cocked his head. "*This* is your job?"

"I know, right? But, yeah, it is."

"Do you intend to work on these websites while in Israel?"

"No. I barely work on them while I'm here in Berlin, to be honest."

He folded his arms. "*Huh.* Fascinating. I'm here all day in the airport asking questions, and some people are just living from their websites. The world is pretty strange, isn't it? Do you think you'd be able to show me these websites?"

"Sure," I replied. BECAUSE I HAD NO CHOICE IF I WANTED TO GO ON HOLIDAY. Levi walked me in the direction of the Hulk. Hulk watched me closely. I thought I saw him lick his lips. I showed Levi my websites on a special EL AL Laptop of Extravagant Paranoia sitting on the countertop near Hulk. Levi went to consult Hulk again, and Hulk shook his head again. I felt as if I were taking part in a game show—The Game of Nations—where everything I said triggered a loud "Wrong!" sound. Levi skipped merrily back to me, a wide grin on his face, as though it were my birthday and he'd prepared strawberry sponge cake.

"Just a few more questions."

I sighed. I'd heard that Israelis were paranoid, but I didn't know they were this paranoid. I just wanted to go on holiday.

"Don't sigh," he said, hurt. "You're doing just fine. We're nearly there. Next question. Where will you stay?"

I retrieved the Airbnb booking from my bag. He held it as if it were sacred. "It says here that the accommodation is for *two* people." He exhaled theatrically, pointing. His face cracked like an egg thrown from a roof terrace.

Gotcha #1. "You told me you were travelling alone!"

We were a team. He had my back. But now... this... Hulk wasn't going to like this. He wasn't going to like this at all.

"I did?" I shifted on the spot. "Well I am *travelling* alone. My girlfriend is on a different flight."

An *egh-ugh* buzzer sounded.

"We're coming back at different times. She's on the Lufthansa flight that left a few hours ago."

He wrote down her name, and took it to Hulk. Hulk didn't move. Trees don't move, either. Neither do walls. Levi bounced back across on the front of his feet. There'd been a few speed bumps on the Yellow Brick Road to check-in, sure, but nothing we couldn't manage if we just worked together and told each other the truth.

"Everything is going great," he lied. "Just one or two more questions. Do you know anyone in Israel? Do you intend to visit the occupied territories?"

I tried to excavate myself from the box marked *irregularity*. "I do not, nor will I. A friend from Tel Aviv did send me a list of recommendations. My girlfriend and I will probably just work through that."

Gotcha #2. The colour drained from his face. "You said you don't know anyone in Israel, yet now I'm hearing you have a list of recommendations from an Israeli friend?!?!"

"I, err, don't..." I stammered. "Well..." I tried to continue. "Erm. The other day I met a girl at a conference. We got talking and I told her I was about to go to Israel and so she sent me this list." I unfolded a piece of A4 paper and handed it to him.

"What is this girl's name?"

I could only remember her first name. This seemed to upset him on a very deep, personal level. I didn't tell him I was actually only 62 percent certain that this was even her first name. The list itself was just a collection of bars and restaurants, with comments like "Be sure to try the eggs Benedict!" I might as well have printed out an Internet listicle called "Seventeen ways to Tel you're in love with Tel Aviv."

Levi checked every word on the list closely, as if deciphering a secret code. He then took the list, the Airbnb booking, and my passport back to Hulk. Hulk shook his head once again.

Seriously? Was I that atypical? With my slightly Israeli face, lack of job, invisible girlfriend, and first-name-only eggs Benedict conference contact?

Levi bounded back like a lamb in a summer's meadow. "We've decided to send you for advanced luggage screening," he said, making it sound as if I'd won an Airport Oscar. "It's nothing to worry about, of course."

It's funny how often people say "it's nothing to worry about" precisely when it's exactly a point in your life deserving of concern. It's like they're trying to convince themselves. It's right up there with other classic human self-denial statements such as "It's just a small lump," "I'll get around to fixing that soon," and, "What you don't know can't hurt you."

Hulk certainly could hurt me. His glances had already been quite bruising; one long, piercing stare had left me winded. Levi disco danced alongside me across the check-in area and over to a metal chair outside an ominous, unmarked door. We were about twenty metres from the—now quite full—check-in area. I was trying to remain calm but found I no longer knew how. I went to where calm was normally stored within me, but everyone there said they'd never heard of it. They recommended I try something called anguish instead. Levi left me on a chair and entered the room.

My brain scurried around unlocking the vaults of my memory, searching through all the things I'd ever done wrong, presumably, so it could confess to these upfront before the waterboarding really got going. It was a long list: I stole a pencil sharpener from a shop when I was twelve; I pretend to be a real journalist to attend sold-out events; I illegally download. Okay, that's quite a short list, but that's only because I've suppressed all the really damning stuff.

Levi returned, retaining his the-Queen-will-see-you-now demeanour. I followed him into the small, windowless space. Inside, a hairy man on an office swivel chair met my gaze as he snapped on a pair of rubber gloves.

"You do that when everyone walks in, right?"

He jutted out his chin and narrowed his eyes.

"I'll just be outside," said Levi jovially, as if dropping off his kid at playschool. "Good luck."

Wait, why would I need luck?

The door closed with a click.

I laughed at the absurdity of all of this.

"Remove your clothes," the man said…

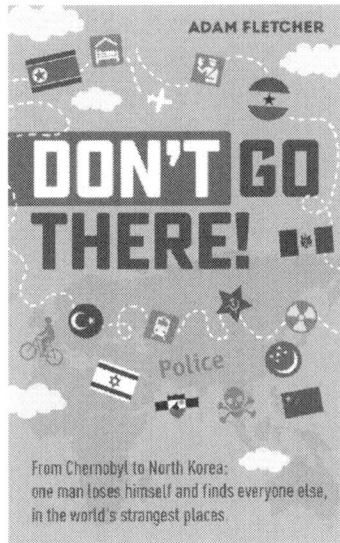

ADAM FLETCHER

DON'T GO THERE!

Police

From Chernobyl to North Korea;
one man loses himself and finds everyone else,
in the world's strangest places.

Does our hero get naked? Does he ever make it Israel? Do worse things happen to him in his adventures in North Korea, Transnistria, Chernobyl, Liberland (the newest country in the world)? Find out today in Don't Go there available at -
https://books2read.com/dont-go-there

Appendix #1 – Case Studies

What follows are a number of case studies from friends and acquaintances that have all achieved the lifestyle, work and location freedom they were looking for. I hope they inspire you or at least suggest that the ideas in this book are not abstract or unrealistic.

Case Study - Christian Jensun - Prenup Online

Problem: The exact cost of getting a prenuptial agreement is unclear, as it often involves negotiations between different lawyers.

Solution: The flat-rate online prenuptial.

Initial financial investment: €150 for online advertising

Months until monthly profit exceeded Freedom Figure: 13

Story: I met Christian (I'm using a pseudonym for both him and his business) in 2011, at a winter retreat for digital nomads. Seven of us spent two months together on an island in Thailand, avoiding the European winter and occasionally, in between long lunches and lazy afternoons at the beach, helping each other with our Internet businesses.

Christian used to work as a lawyer in Denmark. He didn't really like law firms, and if you've had the misfortune to need one, you'll probably know why. He didn't want to graduate and work for a big law firm, and, having always been interested in entrepreneurship, looked for a way to offer legal services online instead. "I noticed that while prenuptials should be simple, because emotions tended to run high during the process, and there is a lot posturing and tense negotiations, it can result in many face-to-face visits to lawyers. For those getting married, it is often hard to tell in advance just how much the whole prenuptial process is going to cost."

So what Christian did is try and convert the service of prenuptials (as I was suggesting earlier in the chapter) into that of a standardised product. Better than that, he turned it into a standardised product that he could sell remotely. No consultations. No face-to-face meetings. No billable hours. Just one flat price.

He registered a simple website, using a free website creation system similar to Wordpress. At the start, his business offered just one product: a fixed-price, all-in-one prenuptial package. The package didn't really exist yet—he would assemble it manually if it turned out people would be willing to arrange their prenuptials online. He then set aside a hundred euros for Google Adwords keywords for the Danish equivalent of "prenuptial online," "cheapest way to get a prenuptial," and "low cost prenup." To his surprise, even with the simple test website he had created and the high price he'd set, people still purchased or made enquiries about the service. Confident it might be profitable enough, he set to work streamlining how exactly he could arrange a prenuptial for people he'd never meet.

He bundled up all the documents you needed to get one into one digital package, breaking the order process into a number of different forms that the customer had to fill in during checkout. The information from these forms then automatically populated blanks on the legal documents Christian needed. He then printed these documents and sent them to the customer. The customer (in this case the two people agreeing to the prenuptial) then signed them.

Of course, this product only worked in simple cases, where consultation and negotiation was not necessary. "This was the biggest challenge in creating the business. The software had to create the legal documents from scratch for each new client. Depending on the clients' answers, different legal sentences are triggered. Some answers will disqualify a client from ordering since the software realises he will need local representation as well." Some still persist in ordering, and these he simply refunds.

Christian is only after the simple cases—not every case. He suggests you do something similar. "Find a pattern of cases that looks repetitive. A good indicator is if older, traditional firms avoid these cases as being too simple or unprofitable, or if some clients actually do the thing you are offering themselves." This is the case with prenuptials, where some couples download free templates and attempt to write their own.

"Simple cases are not as interesting for your established offline competitors. There are not enough billable hours in them, and so they won't try and compete directly with you. But then, as time goes by, you can develop your software to make it work for more and more complex cases, as I have done. By then its really hard for traditional firms to compete because you have such a good head start and far lower costs. They're working manually, while you have a very low cost of production. Even if they match your price—assuming you both charge €100—their cost of production might be €80, while yours will be €5. This means you can spend up to €94 acquiring that customer via advertising while still being profitable, while they have only €19 to spend."

He now helps hundreds of people get prenuptials every month. He's also added a number of additional legal services such as wills and divorces, all sold in the same standardised and fixed-priced way. No exceptions. No special cases.

What really impressed me about Christian is just how analytical he is with his business. Many small business owners, both on and offline, tend to put themselves at the very center of their businesses' processes. They have a big problem outsourcing and delegating. Christian doesn't. In fact, he's almost pathological about this, making it his mission to be as far removed from his business as possible. In addition, he is a relentless a/b tester, endlessly tweaking the copy of his service's website, optimising its funnel to push more people from homepage to order confirmation page.

"A lot of wannabe digital nomads only look for a 100% automatable business. But 90% automated and 10% manual is also okay. Don't be afraid of work. Work is not the enemy—too specialised work is. That's the stuff that's harder to outsource. As long as the 10% manual is not reliant on some hard-to-find key personnel, it's not a problem. The goal is to create your business' systems to survive without you. It's not about impressing some girl you meet at a bar with your 100% automated, zero-effort Internet business."

Over time, Christian has managed to automate and standardise so many of his business' processes that he has now completely removed himself from its day-to-day running. The entire operation is operated by one full-time staff member and three remote workers he's never met, two handling the back office tasks and an East European programmer perfecting the systems that they operate.

Fed up with the politics and high taxation in Denmark, in 2009, Christian moved the business to the island of Malta, where there is almost no corporation tax and low personal income tax, meaning his money goes much further because of his now lower Freedom Figure. On Malta, he lives amongst many Danes who are there for similar reasons.

"If this sort of model works for the legal profession, where trust is everything, it is definitely replicable in other industries. It's just a matter of finding a problem, solving it better than your offline competitors, and not charging too little. I made this mistake for a long time. You have to make sure you leave enough profit for yourself, while still offering your customers value."

Case Study - Jan Schulz-Hofen - Plan.io

Problem: A popular open-source project management system called Redmine requires you to host it on your own server, and can be complex to setup and maintain.

Solution: Plan.io hosts and administers Redmine on your behalf.

Initial Financial Investment: €857. Comprised of €350 server and setup fee, €7 for a website template, €200 for a software as a service payment kit, €300 for a trademark (optional, but Jan highly recommends it), plus 40–50 unpaid eight-hour work days building the initial Plan.io solution and payment system.

Months until monthly profit exceeded Freedom Figure: 24 (but he didn't work full-time on the business until this point, and maintained his consulting income).

Story: Jan is a lifestyle entrepreneur who has a number of small Internet businesses. His main business is an online project management tool called Plan.io. It is, in turn, based on a very popular open source software called Redmine, used by hundreds of thousands of people. People use Redmine to manage complex projects, since you can easily plan tasks and make tickets for people, tracking time and resources. Jan was using it himself for many years to organise his Web agency's client projects.

The problem with Redmine, he found, is that you have to host it yourself (it's open source software). So you need Web space. You need the knowledge to set it up. You have to make backups and set up encryption and email integration. Then there are add-ons to make it do different things, like generating invoices. Sometimes these add-ons change the core Redmine framework. When you come to update this framework in the future, or install security updates, the whole thing becomes a big wobbly mess that you can no longer use or get your data out of.

At first, Jan just tried to fix this problem for himself—to make Redmine more usable for his Web consultancy business. But then, afterwards, happy with his solution, he decided to try and sell it to others. Plan.io looks after your Redmine for you, hosting it, keeping it up to date, applying all the security and bug fixes, and telling you which add-ons you can and can't install. Businesses pay a monthly fee for this service ranging from €9 to €199, depending on how many projects and users they have. Business was slow in the early months, as he didn't invest heavily in advertising. Paying users came, but usually via word of mouth. However, Jan noticed that once people did join, they rarely ever cancelled. His churn rate (the percentage of customers he lost each month) was always just a percent or two. This gave him the confidence to begin investing more heavily in advertising via Google Adwords, even bidding directly for the advertising blocks on Redmine's own homepage.

In those early years, he would invest up to 60 percent of his monthly revenue back into paid advertising in order to grow his user base. "Once you've figured out your Customer Lifetime Value (the total average amount of money a customer will spend with you in total over their whole business lifetime), you know how much you can spend on advertising. Tools like Google Adwords make it easy to see your Customer Acquisition Cost (how much you have to spend to attract that customer in the first place). If your CAC is lower than CLV, you've built a money making machine: Done right, every euro spent can yield €2 or €10 or €20 in return."

Today, thousands of customers pay him a monthly fee for this service. Plan.io's users range from small one- and two-man businesses (I'm also a user) to major multinationals like Allianz, Seagate, and MTV. He learnt how much they depended on the service when, in the very early months of Plan.io, a server hard drive broke and the service was offline for just a few hours. Around 30% of his customers called in, irate.

"In the early days of Plan.io, I had to wear many different hats all the time—sales, phone support, server administrator, accountant, and even occasionally CEO. When the then-only Plan.io server went offline, I was sweating blood partitioning hard drives and re-initializing RAID arrays while trying to remain calm, with the phone ringing nonstop and my inbox flooded with support requests. Our clients were so afraid that we had lost their important business data that some would shout at me over the phone and say the most inappropriate things. I was able to recover the server within hours, not losing a single file in the process. But at that moment I realized that Plan.io had grown from side project to a real business on which others rely—and expect to be able to rely upon."

Plan.io was a business that scaled, but it was also offering a critical productivity tool to its users. It could simply never break, never go offline, and never lose any of its data. The technical infrastructure that underpinned it had to be bulletproof. So Jan took a leap of faith and re-invested almost all of his monthly Plan.io income to hire more specialised system admins and programmers to support him. He bought more servers to provide full redundancy, and he brought in a customer service employee to help and train new customers. Today, the whole team counts 10 staff members.

Unlike Christian, and because of the more complicated and specialised nature of Plan.io's business, Jan has found it difficult to remove himself from Plan.io's day-to-day running. Increasingly stressed, and with not enough time to invest in his other projects and interests (he still has the digital agency, and also a co-working space), he set himself a challenge—within one year, he had to simplify all of the businesses so that they ran without his day-to-day involvement, and, more importantly, without his physical presence. He wanted to be location-free. If he succeeded, he would join me in Mexico for a winter retreat. It was a larger project than he expected, since so many of his businesses' processes needed to be redesigned, simplified, and outsourced, but he succeeded with a few weeks to spare.

Today, Plan.io is going from strength to strength. Jan still works harder than most of the Berlin lifestyle entrepreneurs I know—easily 50+ hours a week—and is certainly the most passionate about his business, but now he can do it from anywhere. His advice for people who'd like to do the same is "be your own best customer. I used Plan.io myself first to organize my daily work as a consultant. When Plan.io's customer base grew and we needed a software to manage customer support, we designed an app that would integrate that with the overall workflow in Plan.io. When I decided that I wanted to be able to run the business remotely, we developed a chat app that could help our team overcome the fact that we're not sitting in the same room all the time. It is in fact the best way of creating your own business: Find a common problem that you and others actually have. Make sure it's a problem you deeply understand, and for which others are willing to pay for a solution. Then go on and solve it."

Problem: Hotels do not have the time and expertise to manage their social media presence.

Solution: A social media and online review management business, sold as a monthly subscription.

Initial Investment: €100 + time—*a lot of time.*

Months until monthly profit exceeded Freedom Figure: 18

Story: Often, when Jan and I would meet of an evening, he'd tell me that although his long-term goal was location freedom, he wouldn't really be able to enjoy that independence unless his girlfriend, Kirsten, also became location-free, and would be able to travel with him. For the past eight years, Kirsten had a full-time job at a hotel—a job, which, while secure, came with anti-social hours and low pay, as is often the case with the hospitality industry. With no further possibility for promotion and a job that no longer provided an intellectual challenge, it was time for a change. After slow but steady pressure and reassurance from Jan about the joys of self-employment, she decided to give it a go, knowing that the risks were not all that high. Even if it failed, she knew the hospitality industry so well by now that she was sure she could get a similar job again.

For her own business, she just needed to find a suitable problem. She started by looking at the specific tasks that she did each day at the hotel. After many years in the hotel industry, she had a good idea what hotels were good at, and where they struggled. She knew that hoteliers tend to be rather traditional, and they often don't have a good understanding of the Internet. "I knew how often my friends, and hotel guests, and I checked review websites before booking. But I also knew that hotels often lacked the time and expertise to monitor, respond, and optimise their presence on these websites."

So Kirsten decided to design a business offering just this one service—online review management for hotels. She called it ReviewPartner. ReviewPartner maintains her hotel customers' Facebook pages and monitors all the major review sites such as Yelp and Tripadvisor. ReviewPartner responds directly to reviews for its hotels (both positive and negative), making sure guests are as satisfied and reassured as possible. Potential guests then see how proactive and committed the hotels are in responding to online reviews and queries, and so feel more confident about staying there.

Not wanting to invest too much money in the business in the early stages, before the idea had been validated, she began by purchasing a simple €20 website template theme from one of the many online website theme marketplaces. She then asked a graphic designer friend to customise it slightly for her, and create her own logo. Since she didn't have any HTML or design skills, the website would be Wordpress, which allowed her to change the content easily. A few weeks later, after investing many hours but almost no money, the service went online. "While the business didn't really require any money to start, I paid in other ways. I never imagined that I'd start my own business one day, and it took a lot of courage, nerves, lost sleep, giving up my job, and being willing to live from my savings for as long as it took to earn money from the business. Of course, I don't regret it, but it was still an incredibly stressful time."

The only way she could relax then was to throw herself into her fledgling business. She worked long hours, cold calling hotels in search of her first customer. The sales process took longer than she expected, but she found the first customer almost immediately, within the first week. The second signed up just a day later. She couldn't believe it. Since her solution is sold via monthly subscription (in a number of different packages ranging from €149 to €349), even if it takes many hours to find a customer, once they are signed up, they deliver revenue each month without further selling required.

After this great start, she went several weeks with no new customers. She was on the phone all day, which she hated, but she stuck with it. "This time period was an absolute rollercoaster. For the first time, I was not part of a team, so I had to motivate myself alone. Many people showed interest in the service, and this gave me confidence, but then I'd invest a lot of time with them and they'd not sign, for whatever reason. I learnt a lot about myself during this phase: how I tick, how to stay motivated, and that you won't have great success every day. Solid foundations are built slowly."

Kirsten persevered, learning whom she needed to speak to and how to best sell the merits of the ReviewPartner service. Once she knew which features to showcase, and which size of hotels were attracted to it, she cut back on the cold calls and hired a remote worker by the hour to help her identify high-potential hotels. Then she began using a mixture of cold calls, emails, and postal marketing to reach them. It was a long slog, but, just like Jan and Plan.io, she found that, once the customers joined, they simply didn't cancel. They loved the service, and many hoteliers actually recommend it to their fellow hoteliers. Within nine months, she'd matched 80% of her income from her full-time job. "To be honest, this was far faster than I imagined. I was still stressed and nervous about the future of the business, but I started to believe it had long-term potential."

Today, some two years later, she's not rich, nor likely to become it. But she is now exceeding her previous salary. "For me, it was never about having a startup or getting rich. I just wanted more time and flexibility, while also having a somewhat stable income." Now she has a job she can do from anywhere, and that she's passionate about. She's her own boss. She's not reliant on a single employer for her income. She has no staff to manage (just the occasional remote worker). No offices. No night shifts. No weekends. It's just her and her laptop.

While the business is unlikely to scale into a much larger operation, she also doesn't want it to. It's a lifestyle business. Even if a customer does cancel, which is very rare, she doesn't need to worry, since her income is spread across many more. Sometimes it's very busy and she has a lot of work to do; other times it's quiet and she can stop working and go do something more fun, knowing that she can always check email or be reached via her phone if anything urgent happens. "Of course it's good when your job is your passion, but I have many interests, and becoming self-employed was primarily about creating enough time for them. I think work should pay for our lifestyles and, where possible, also be fun, but not be all-consuming."

In fact, so confident did she feel about being able to run this business remotely that, at the end of the business' first year, she joined Jan and me in Mexico. Since then, they've done many long trips together, mixing travel and remote working. I think Kirsten's story is particularly inspiring because she doesn't fit the traditional model of a solo entrepreneur. She's not a big risk taker. She's not experienced in building websites or running her own business. She started with what she knew best, researched a problem, and sold the solution in a simple, scalable, repeat income way. "I hope that my story shows that it's possible for anyone, if they're willing to take some risks and work really hard, to create a job that they enjoy, and that gives them the lifestyle they want. It's not easy, but then nothing worthwhile ever is. It's good to listen to advice, and to meet people who have done what you want to do. But, ultimately, we're all different, and you need to find your way to whatever it is that you want."

Problem: Students need to compile their notes from a wide range of sources—textbooks, journal articles, lectures.

Solution: Instead of spending time chasing sources, wouldn't it be better to obtain a complete set of notes and spend that time learning them? Oxbridge Notes is a platform that allows students to sell their notes to other students.

Initial Investment: Two weeks and €100 in advertising.

Months until monthly profit exceeded Freedom Figure: Approx 60% reached within two months, but it took him two years until he stopped supplementing his income with freelance work.

Story: Just like Christian and Jan, Jack's business was also born out of personal experience and frustration. Jack studied law, and by the time he graduated, just like Christian he "reeled at the prospect of a life working in Big Law, of depleting my entire youth chained to a desk and surrounded by people who would agree to that same kind of life choice." Instead, he wanted "a life filled with adventure, one where I couldn't predict what I'd be doing in one, three, or five years' time."

While studying law at Oxford, Jack was surprised at just how many folders of immaculately prepared outlines, notes from lectures, and summaries from the chapters of expensive legal textbooks he was creating. "By the time I graduated, I had over 1000 pages of notes, and that was considered terse." A good student, many people complimented him on his notes, and begged, borrowed, and, on one occasion, actually stole them from him before exams. This gave him an idea… "I was always fascinated by businesses that sell something that's free for you to supply incremental units of. Mostly digital items—for example, digital sheet music, stock photos, ebooks, etc. It dawned on me that perhaps my notes might be a member of this high-rolling club."

Some quick online research revealed the existence of a few websites in other countries that allowed students to sell their notes to other students. Students wanted to pass their exams. Notes are highly condensed information that empowers people to pass exams. Plus, if you've already invested £9k a year in tuition fees (as is the case in England), would you really balk at paying another €49 for the exam notes of an A-grade student who sat the exact test you're studying for just the previous year? Jack suspected that many students wouldn't.

Jack had been slowing teaching himself how to program over the previous year, and so created a simple HTML/CSS website called Oxbridge Notes (Oxbridge is a common moniker combining Oxford and Cambridge, the two most famous English universities). After the site was online, just as Christian had done, Jack first tested demand with Google and Facebook ads that directed people to his site. To his surprise, he saw good sales soon after switching on the advertising. "There was no competition in this niche five years ago, so advertising was dirt cheap, which allowed the business to grow quickly."

After a few months of sales, he felt confident that the business had potential and immediately set about improving the look and feel of the website. He also contacted his friends at Oxford and offered them a 50% commissions deal for sales on their notes. Over time, he moved on to other universities and other courses. More Google and Facebook ads, more sales, further investment. Piece by piece, note by notes, he slowly built the service up, investing heavily in advertising and automation. "Each time I want to add a new topic, I try and get one set of A-grade notes, and then I can expand out once I know there's demand. Today, I'm proud to say that Oxbridge Notes has exam notes for hundreds of subjects, and is used by thousands of students each year to help them prepare for their exams."

It takes him a lot of work to find the right notes, but once they are in the system they might sell hundreds of times without him having to do anything at all, as the notes are delivered automatically to the buyers via PDF. Now, five years later, the day-to-day management is handled by a remote worker paid per hour, following meticulous process documents created by Jack and this employee that explain nearly every scenario and how to respond to it. Jack has now expanded the business to other countries like Australia and the USA, and works 10–15 hours a week, mostly programming new features. Since it's all online, he's also location-free. The rest of the time he writes music and follows his various interests from his new base in Berlin.

For people who would like to build a similar lifestyle, he says the key is "Leveraging freedoms. Attaining one freedom (e.g., of location or from long hours), then leveraging that from the others. For example, if you move to a country with a lower costs of living, you need to work less hours. There's your first freedom. Next, you can invest those newly gained hours into building skills that will free you from having a boss, or having to work from a specific location, and so on and so forth. The most important step is to secure that first initial freedom.[74]"

Case Study - Fabian Dittrich - Zendesk and Helpando.it

Skill: Customer service specialist

Weekly hours: 40+

Location: Planet Earth (for now)

Story: Fabian Dittrich is an avid traveller. Whether it's spending a year travelling through Africa, traversing South America in a Land Rover, or spending months in the jungle helping a sick friend visit a shaman, the one thing Fabian really loves is being on the move. So, it was always going to be hard for him to find a job that would accommodate his wanderlust. Surprisingly, however, he did, working as a consultant for Zendesk, an online customer service tool. Rather than seeing his nomadic nature as a threat, Zendesk embraced it. In fact, in just 18 months, Fabian flew 110 times for Zendesk on business trips, travelling to different cities to give customer boot camps in European capitals, demonstrating Zendesk technology and helping new customers get set up and migrate across from competitor products. He'd schedule these trips to give him some free time to explore new places. "If, for example, I would do a training session in Barcelona, I'd try to put it on a Thursday, then work Friday and the next Monday from Barcelona, and using my free time to check out the city."

Almost all of his job could be done remotely. So when he didn't have a boot camp to run, it didn't matter where he was. As time went on and Zendesk's trust in him increased, he was spending more and more time on the road.

Fabian thought he'd found his dream job. Not that it wasn't hard work—often the 40-hour workweek he was contracted for became more like 70 hours. First thing in the morning he'd wake up, take his laptop from the bedside table, and, regardless of where he was, start working. The end of the evening was the same process, only reversed. This is of course the danger of remote working: Because you can do it from anywhere, whenever, if you're not careful, you can end up doing it from everywhere, always.

"At one point I wanted to have the balance back, travel more, have more adventures again. I took my whole year's holiday in December 2012 and worked as a guide and translator for a sick friend who wanted to go to the Amazon and see a shaman. There, in a jungle wood house, listening to the noise the heavy rain produces on the wood roof, it came to me: This is where I am most alive—on the road, embracing the unknown."

So Fabian talked to Zendesk about working less days a week so that he could travel more. To his surprise, instead, they encouraged him to found his own company—an online solutions business that would work with Zendesk technology and customers. They even referred him many of his early clients. Helpando.it was born. "It's not the typical digital nomad story of doing a website or graphic design project here and there while drinking cocktails from a beach in Bali. Today, Helpando.it comprises 10 freelancers and helps US clients from banks to tech startups like Skyscanner, Fox, and Spilgames implement Zendesk's technology. We are doing all that on the move."

In fact, Fabian is so passionate about entrepreneurship and flexible working that, with two friends, he's bought an old Land Rover and is managing Helpando.it from the road, driving through South America for his new project called StartupDiaries.org. They plan to meet freelancers, startup entrepreneurs, and lifestyle designers and document their way of working. "The way we work is changing. More and more people are working independent of time, place, and corporate organisations, crafting an alternative lifestyle that's better for our own souls, our loved ones, and possibly our planet. I want to help promote that so that we can all get there faster."

Case Study - Bryce Pedersen - Marketing Manager

Skill: Brand management

Weekly hours: 40+

Location: Berlin, Germany

Story: Just like Fabian, Bryce and the international company he works for are good role models for employee/employer relationships in the digital age. Bryce works for the startup CastLabs, streaming video specialists. CastLabs are progressive enough to not require their staff to be physically present at any of their offices around the world, but have employees dotted all over the globe, with most meetings taking place via Skype. In fact, this was how he was hired. "There I was, a Canadian living in Berlin, having a Skype interview with the German managing director in Brazil. I had never met the man, and only knew what he looked like from a picture I managed to find online. This was the first moment in my career I had encountered the new-world employment mentality of geographical borders being outright irrelevant."

Staff are encouraged to travel and meet their colleagues when possible, and in cities where they have offices they even rent long-term spare apartments so that travelling staff members have somewhere to stay. Like at many tech startups, the staff have a lot of work to do, and tend to work long hours, but they are empowered to work when and where they like. "Our company's culture is different from what is currently the norm. We have an extremely low amount of micromanagement, which leads to a lot of individual responsibility. I would argue that the employee empowerment afforded to us has a psychological effect that the organisation benefits from: It often causes us to push ourselves further to reach a degree of quality we are personally satisfied with. I do not think this output is as easy to elicit from an employee with a typical nine-to-five job."

Bryce has also been willing to move to find opportunities, having worked in Canada, Dublin, London, and now Berlin. What Bryce does well—and this is why he's always in demand—is combining a specialism with several in-demand generalisms. "Marketing is my core focus, but I have also taught myself how to program and use graphic design software. While I cannot replace a fully specialized software developer or designer at an ad agency, I can take on aspects of their work, such as building websites, and my value to an employer is increased as a result. Also, as I work for a software company, understanding programming is quite beneficial to working with my developer colleagues."

Aware that startup companies are volatile by nature, Bryce has been working to establish himself as an expert in the streaming video industry, writing articles for trade publications and regularly travelling to attend industry conferences. "Job security does not exist in the same manner as it did 50 years ago; so being mobile and networking within your industry is essential. Finding a job you really enjoy is tough. For some, they may never find one. But working is such a large part of your life, I think it's worth all of the uncertainty and effort to find something that makes you happy. It's easier to move to another country for work than most people realize. It takes a bit of legwork, but looking for jobs outside of your home country can provide you with more opportunities. If you're willing to travel, there's a world of opportunity for you."

Case Study - Manuel Meurer - Freelance Programmer

Skill: Ruby on Rails programmer

Years as freelancer: 5

Weekly hours billed: 20

Location: Berlin, Germany

Story: Manuel lives in Berlin and works three days a week for a major media company as a freelance programmer. He doesn't use remote working sites like Upwork, but mostly finds his clients via networking and word of mouth. The programming framework he works with is called Ruby on Rails, and is, at present, a highly in-demand skill, requested by many of the city's startups.

Because of this high demand, an experienced, freelance Ruby on Rails programmer can command around €500 a day. In a city in which you can live very comfortably for €1500 a month, it makes little sense to be an employed programmer and give up that many hours of your week.

While Manuel enjoys client projects, he is mostly interested in building his own business. So he uses his freelance income as a financial base, and the other two days a week he invests in ProductWidgets.com, his online service for matching website visitors with targeted affiliate product recommendations. Many programmers in Berlin work this way. Client work pays the bills, they do just enough of it as necessary, and invest the rest of their time building their own things, with the long-term goal of ending their contract work.

Manuel is aware that the boom on Ruby on Rails probably won't last. He has already re-trained himself from now-less-in-demand programming languages like php and java, to exclusively focus on

Ruby on Rails. This allows him to maximise the returns of this specialism today, and respond to the market. If the rates drop because a new technology becomes the de-facto Berlin startup standard, or because more and more people reach his competency level in Ruby on Rails, he can move to a new technology.

The other really important thing for Manuel is that being a freelancer allows him to be selective in which client work he takes. "Recently, I was invited to take part in the project of a major telecoms company. The kick-off meeting was a full day long, in which I got to meet different departments of the company. Over a period of three years, this company had invested over 100 million euros in a major IT project that had now stalled. My job would be to take it over and lead a small IT team to deploy and train the telecom's staff on how to use it. On paper, it sounded like a good project, with a very high budget." However, when I saw him the evening after the kick-off meeting, his opinion had changed. Apparently the whole day had been spent playing referee to an inter-departmental boxing match.

"Team A hated Team B and blamed them for the project's failure. Team B blamed Team A. None of the system's potential users wanted to have a new system to learn, and they were all actively opposing its deployment. The management team was willing to blame anyone and everyone except themselves." Everyone's advice was to abandon the old system entirely—the system that cost 100 million euros—and just start again. However, since that would mean they'd have wasted 100 million euros, Manuel was told that his new system should interface to the older, inferior system. It didn't need to actually *use* that old system—which by now was out-of-date and irrelevant anyway—but it should just *connect to it* so that the management team could convince the board of directors that the investment had been worthwhile, and that this new system leveraged the old one in some useful but really just entirely fictitious way.

Manuel said, "Thanks, but no thanks." That evening, over a beer, we celebrated. "Today reminded me what it's like to be an employee," he said. "Being able to say no to projects like that is exactly why I became a freelancer. That project is a widow maker."

Case Study - Frederik Eichelbaum - Futurist

Skills: Strategy. Futurism. Music composition.

Years as freelancer: 5

Weekly hours billed: 30

Location: Berlin, Germany

Story: Sometimes you meet people and it's very hard for you to imagine them working as full-time employees. Their interests are too broad, and they tend to flit between many different ideas and disciplines, like drunk wasps might flowers. Unless they could find an extremely diverse full-time position, committing to just one profession would clip their multifaceted wings. Frederik Eichelbaum is one of those people. Fred's interested in just about everything, but mostly music, literature, science, and futures research (which is what he studied). He is very much a renaissance man, well versed in many different disciplines without being a true specialist in any one.

"The idea of financial security and a stable income has never excited me. The classic mortgage-financed house, the pension plans, the career moves that you need to make look like a straight line of incremental achievements leading to a single professional calling—I neither want, nor need my life to be that structured."

Currently, Fred juggles several different work projects. He works as a freelancer four hours a day, as a curator for technology conference company *hy!* He then devotes another few hours a day to writing research reports about the potential of new technological breakthroughs for R&D departments of major German companies via a digital research company called Hypermorgen that he started with a few university friends.

It's also left him time to try founding his own business. Living in Berlin, and seeing the influx of highly skilled foreigners to Berlin, he spotted an opportunity. "Many foreigners move to Germany without being able to speak German, and so need help with research and administrative tasks. They're also shocked at how low levels of customer service are here. So I started Zipster.co, a small business supplying high-quality, German-speaking virtual assistants."

What I also find really smart about how Fred has structured his work is that not only is his day-to-day very diverse, which stops him getting bored, but all his projects benefit and support each other. His work at Hypermorgen introduces him to swaths of interesting people that he can then book for *hy!* conferences. The people that attend and speak at these conferences are often perfect candidates to benefit from one of the Zipster's remote workers. The larger his network becomes, the more all of his projects benefit.

Fred is a good example of how, by combining different generalists skills and not limiting yourself to one interest area, you can still produce a reliable monthly income with spare time to indulge your passions.

"Of course, at first, this path is a lot less forgiving, but once it starts working out, it really gives back. You start feeling very resilient and don't make your choices based on fear anymore. That's an invaluable psychological asset to me, for which I gladly forego the money I didn't earn because of not choosing regular employment in those first few years. I love how varied my days are, and that I can follow my interests down whatever weird rabbit holes they lead me."

Case Study - Siobhan Gallagher - Freelance Editor

Skills: Copyediting. Structural editing. Revision/Ghostwriting

Years as a freelancer: 7

Weekly hours billed: 25–35

Location: Martizay, France

Story: In 2012, I decided to self-publish my first novel. But rather than trying to do everything myself, I outsourced all the various parts to Upwork remote workers. I hired a graphic designer for the cover, a typesetter for the layout, a conversion specialist to prepare all the different eBook formats, and lastly, Siobhan, an editor/proofreader. Siobhan is an American now living in rural France. Previously, she had worked for a number of Fortune 100 financial firms and a Wall Street brokerage, but she became increasingly disillusioned with corporate working conditions and the long hours with no overtime. "Doing more with less" became the industry mantra, which is management-speak for "work more without getting paid more."

In her case, it was her editing skills that set her apart from her peers. Editing is an often unappreciated but vital skill. She found that the longer she stayed in her position, the more bloated her tasks got and the more she detested being embroiled in the daily politics of the organisation. As a result, work became a tedious chore and she found herself spending less and less time doing the kind of work that she loved and was really good at.

Disillusioned, she decided to quit corporate America altogether in favour of doing the kind of writing she enjoyed. Not content with that major lifestyle change, she sold her house, car, and most of her possessions and relocated entirely, moving around Europe for three years with her two small dogs until finally settling in rural France, where she could pay cash for a home and live for a fraction of the money she needed to survive in the US. But she couldn't afford to retire in her forties. There was just one problem: "It's impossible to get a job here in France if you're not fluent in French, which I'm not," she confessed. "It was critical for me to network globally in order to garner sufficient clients to make a reasonable living."

A friend and professor at the University of Vienna tipped her off to the remote working service Upwork. Within hours, she had begun advertising her writing and editing services, which was how I found her. "There is such a wealth of work on Upwork," she said. "Since getting my foot in the door and working for peanuts to establish my reputation, I've increased my hourly rate six-fold in the course of four years, and no one's complained when my rates have gone up. Instead, the caliber of my clientele has improved dramatically. I've scored client heavyweights I never would have crossed paths with if it hadn't been for Upwork."

Working with her on my first book was a joy. Her experience was evident in everything she edited. Stories I sent her came back cleaner, leaner, and funnier. She even added humour to some of them. Every time she completes a project for an Upwork client, they are encouraged to leave public feedback on her performance. Her performance has been so good and so consistent that she's now booked up months in advance, with most of her clients now being publishers vs. authors. Even better, there's no politics, no meetings, no two-hour-each-way New York City commute, no staff management, and no bosses. It's just her calling the shots. She decides what projects to take, what timelines are realistic, and how much money she wants. While she arguably works as many hours as she did before, she's much, much happier—those hours are spent much more enjoyably because they're spent doing what she loves to do, and what she does best. She's not financially dependent on one company. Instead, her income is spread across the hundreds of people like me who contract for her services. The higher she maintains her average rating at Upwork (it's ranged between 4.98 and the maximum achievable 5.0 since she scored her first rating), the higher the hourly rate she can demand. And the flexibility is enviable. She can travel when she wants for as long as she wants, whether it's across Europe or to the US to visit family, while continuing to work remotely. "I have a portable life, no question," she admits. "I don't have to jam my vacation into one or two precious weeks every year, like I did back in the US. Now I spend winters in Portugal—three or four months—and often pick up and spend five or six weeks in all sorts of places in Europe. So being able to work from anywhere is not only a huge advantage, it's imperative. I couldn't afford to travel the way I do for extended periods without the freedom and facility to work when I want to work. All I need is the Internet."

Siobhan is now one of Upwork's most in-demand editors, and loves the flexibility of her new lifestyle. "I can't even imagine myself doing anything else now."

Appendix #2 - Build an Internet Business in Six Steps

I've devised a basic six-step template that can (hopefully) be followed to learn the basics en route to Internet-fuelled, passive self-employment. Because it's quite detailed, and so not likely to be interesting for most readers, it's out here in the Appendix.

Now, to preface this, there's a good chance you won't be right the first time with your business idea—that what you really need to offer is something just slightly different to what you will first attempt to sell. Don't worry about that—it's completely normal. It's an iterative process of developing and testing hunches. The faster you can do this, the more cheaply you can do it, and the better off you will be. Remember the important things discussed in earlier chapters that will support you during this potentially long (like, years-long) process—keep your cost of living low; the best marketer wins, not the best idea; failure is expected; trust in systems, not goals.

Since the specific tools and services you should be using are always changing, I won't focus on those too much. They'll only go out of date. Instead, I'll talk of the underlying principles involved in each step.

Let's begin...

Step 1. The Problem

Definition - The problem is the specific inconvenience, or societal need, that you are going to fill with your scalable product/service.

By the time we are finished diagnosing it, you should be able to formulate your problem in just one sentence—a sentence that anyone can understand, whether they have the specific problem or not.

Finding a Problem

The smaller the problem, the better. We only need one tiny inconvenience, one broken process from everyday life. We're not trying to build the next Google—just a lifestyle business. Start small and stay small. In order to find a problem, it's easiest to begin with our own lives. A notepad is your friend here, your pocket its bedfellow. Keep one in there at all times, and, any moment you can't find some information, can't find a product or service when you need one, or just notice something that frustrates you because of its inefficiency, you are going to write it down.

Each one of these is a friction point that we can try and solve with a clever solution. Here are a few mostly stupid problems I've noticed in the past day:

- Gloves are easy to lose.
- It's hard to find the light switch in the dark.
- Shins connect easily to furniture (see: *it's hard to find the light switch in the dark*).
- There's not much English language information online about registering and closing businesses in Germany.
- Neither Lonely Planet nor Rough Guide have dedicated travel guides for Ghana.
- Most people want a pet, but not the responsibility of looking after a pet.

Is there a business in any of those? Probably not. Who knows? I wouldn't try any of them, because I'm not really passionate about fixing any of these problems. But they might be worth researching further. Usually, instead, it's best to start looking for problems in the areas you know best or are most interested in—which is often the same. It was my experience at Spreadshirt that gave me the knowledge and contacts to create both TheTeeDirectory and The Hipstery.

Everyone is an expert at something. What topic so fascinates you that you could discuss it for hours? Look at your bookshelf. What topics appear there again and again in the books you own? If a friend of yours was on *Who Wants to be a Millionaire* and stuck on a question, what type of question would it have to be for them to immediately want to call you for help? *Start there.*

If you're still struggling to find a good problem, the best idea to talk to as many different people as possible. Ask them what they do for a living. Ask them to describe their days. Ask them to tell you the parts they hate about what they do. Ask them what one thing would make their work life easier. Ask them how many people they know with that same problem. Then you can go away and create a plan for solving it. Bring it back to them, and ask them if it solves it. Ask them, if the solution existed, would they pay for it? What's important here is that we are collecting feedback, and as detailed a definition of the problem as we possibly can.

If we don't want to talk to people in person, we can use email or Facebook, or read forums or blogs. If anything, the problem is that there are too many potential problems, not too few—it's just a question of training ourselves to spot them, formulate them, and research them.

Step 2. The Solution

Definition - The solution is the product/service you are going to offer to solve the problem.

Characteristics of Good Solutions

They improve on existing solutions. Ideally, what you are looking to create is a *better way* to do something that already exists. That way, you already know there is a demand for the service. Airbnb is not a new idea, it's just a smarter, more scalable online travel/holiday letting agent. That's why it works. It takes an old solution—letting and holiday apartment agents—and creates something that scales better and is more efficient for the people that use it. We can see many photos of the properties. We can read reviews from people who have stayed there. We don't have to leave our houses and talk to actual humans. Below are some Internet startups that have improved upon existing solutions to create business for themselves. (Your business will be much smaller. These are just well-known examples.):

A: Problem / B: Pre-Internet Solution / C: Post-Internet Improved Solution

A: It's hard to find high quality content to watch. / B: Pay TV / C: Pay TV + one low fee, cancel anytime, stream-able to all your devices = *Netflix*

A: I want to listen to my music on the move. / B: Portable music players / C: Mp3 players + one low fee, cancel anytime, listen to as much music as you like, sync across all your devices = *Spotify*

A: Hotels are boring and don't have amenities like a kitchen. / B: Holiday apartments/ apartment brokers / C: Letting agents + central platform linking renter and rentees, with quality photography, ratings, and review = *Airbnb*

A: I need to get somewhere fast and I don't have a car. / B: Taxis / C: Taxis + automatic payments, reviews, and ratings = *Uber*

A: I like clothes shopping but I hate clothes shops. / B: Mail-order catalogues / C: Mail order catalogues + e-commerce and free returns via normal mail = *Zalando*

A: I want to buy original gifts that you can't find in every store. / B: Flea markets and specialist stores / C: Flea markets + personal connection to product creators, greater range of products, orderable from home = *Dawanda*

A: I like trying new cosmetics, but not keeping track of what new cosmetics are out there. / B: Mail-order cosmetic catalogues (e.g., Avon) / C: Cosmetics + monthly subscription and chance to try and give feedback about newest cosmetics products = *Glossybox*.

They scale.

Solutions where you have to do a long consultation with the customer to convince them to buy, or where you would need to be physically present, don't scale very well, which is why we're trying to move from services (like letting agents, lawyers, or language teachers) to digital information products that can be made once but sold repeatedly, with minimal extra effort per sale: ebooks, online video courses, templates, guides, marketplaces, affiliate products, etc.

They have repeat revenue potential.

You are going to do a lot of work and spend a lot of money on marketing to find your customers. It's great if, after investing all that effort, you have not a one-off solution to sell them, but a solution sold by subscription. It's like the difference between selling one piece of gym equipment and selling a gym membership that auto-renews each month. Where applicable, it would be great if you could find a way to offer your solution by subscription.

Dollarshaveclub.com is a nice example. They sell an incredible commoditized product—razor blades, but as a monthly subscription, starting at just $3 a month. They currently sell more than 24 million razor blades this way each year. They have to work hard to find a customer, but once they do, their (cancel anytime) subscription allows them to keep making money from that customer month after month.

They can be tested easily/cheaply.

At the beginning, you have only a hunch about how many people have the problem and how much they'd be willing to pay you to fix it. Because of this, you need a solution that allows you to test that hunch for as little effort and money as possible. Ways to do this:

1. Put up a simple website for your service/product, as if that product already exists. Then reach out to potential customers and get their feedback. See how many try to buy it or provide their email addresses for the chance to buy it later. Alternatively, proactively contacting potential customers before you start is a great idea.

2. If it's a product, you could consider crowdsourcing the money you need through websites like Kickstarter, Indiegogo, or Seed Match. Here you can share your idea with people all over the world who can pledge money to you that allow you to go out and create it, should enough people think it is a good idea.

If the solution you want to build seems too big for you to handle, and too hard to test demand for, you should think of it like a cake—accept that you can't eat the whole thing and slice it into smaller and smaller pieces. Focus on the slice where you can add the most value for the lowest initial investment. Keep that part. Mercilessly cut away everything else.

Step 3. The Buying Cycle

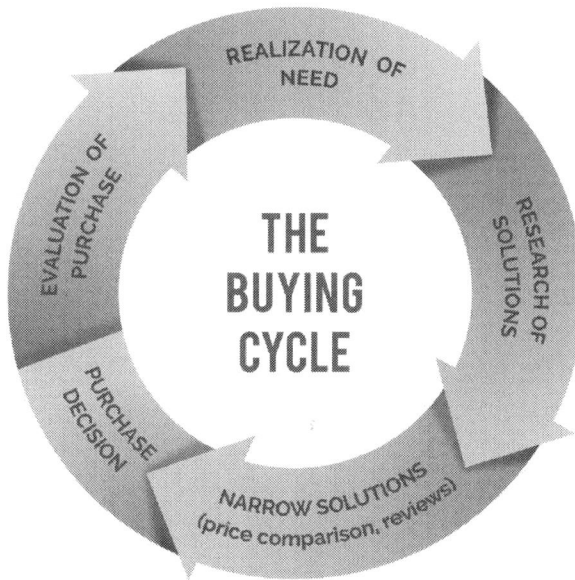

Definition - The process your would-be customers go through when buying the product/service you are offering.

Think about how you buy something, like, say, a travel guide for Ghana. Usually, you don't just realise one day that you know very little about Ghana, walk yourself to the nearest shop that has books, and then purchase the first one your eyes fall upon. Some people might do this, and good luck to them, but the vast majority of people will not. Instead, they pass through what is called a *buying cycle*.

A: Buying Cycle Stage / B: Customer's Action

A: Awareness of Needs / B: We book a holiday to Ghana and realise we need to plan the trip.

A: Assessment of Alternatives / B: We look around either online or offline to see what guides exist.

A: Alleviation of Risk / B: We create a shortlist, perhaps check some blogs, asking friends, reading review sites or the reviews on Amazon.

A: Decision / B: Purchase (either on or offline).

A: Achievement of Results / B: Book arrives, trip can be planned.

What is the buying cycle for your proposed product/service?

This same cycle is occurring with pretty much every product or service, from *Which restaurant shall we go to this evening?* to *What should be our next car?* The better we can identify the cycle for your product/service, and where the people go at each stage, the better we can position your solution and encourage them to buy it from you, and not from your competitors. As a solutions provider, you can even theoretically create something to sell at every stage of the cycle. Keeping with the Ghana guide example:

A: Buying Cycle Stage / B: Potential Solution You Can offer / C: Business Model of Solution

A: Awareness of Needs / B: *Ghanaeverything.com* – After we've been to Ghana, we'll know a lot about it and could put that knowledge to work on a dedicated site offering travel advice for it. / C: Selling of ebook/trip itineraries/hotel recommendations.

A: Assessment of Alternatives / B: *Ghanabookreviews.com* - A review website comparing all the existing books about the country. / C: Affiliate commission/paid membership/advertising.

A: Alleviation of Risk / B: A price comparison site (very likely just a featured offered on ghanabookreviews rather than a separate service / C: Affiliate commission/ advertising.

A: Decision / B: Ghanabooks.*com* - An ecommerce store where people can buy books. / C: E-commerce

Which part of the buying cycle should your solution target?

Here we have a trade off. The earlier stages in the cycle allow you to sell information, and as we learnt from TheTeeDirectory, information scales really well. It's where you're most likely to build a passive business. But the earlier you are in the buying cycle, the more often you have to push the customer through the rest of it, educating them on what to buy, why they should buy it, and where to buy it from. The more stages before they will actually buy something, the more likely it is that they will drop out, or discover one of your competitors along the way and buy from them instead.

With TheTeeDirectory, my solution was to try and build one platform that would cover as much of the "I want to buy a new t-shirt" buying cycle as possible, so that once people arrived, ideally, they wouldn't need to leave until they were ready to buy at one of the 500 stores I had listed, clicking my affiliate links on the way.

A: Buying Cycle Stage / B: Customer's Action / C: TeeDirectory's Solution

A: Awareness of Needs / B: Google t-shirt-related search term (e.g., "batman t-shirt germany"). / C: Customised t-shirt search engine showing all batman t-shirts across all stores featured in directory.

A: Assessment of Alternatives / B: Find store where price and style match my needs. / C: Filtering by colour, price, and location.

A: Alleviation of Risk / B: Check for customer reviews. / C: Every store featured has customer reviews evaluating the store by quality, delivery time, speed, and a range of other factors. Some stores have dozens and dozens of customer reviews.

A: Decision / B: Price comparison coupons or special offers? / C: Every store has a special offer and coupon code section. The stores could add these themselves, or we added them manually. The customer could check the offers and automatically copy the coupon codes with one click.

A: Achievement of Results / B: Redirected to store to buy the t-shirt. / C: Leave a small toolbar at the top of the customer's browser window after they pass through to one of the stores. This thanks them for visiting and encourages them to follow us on Facebook/join our newsletter list so that we can market offers to them at a later point in time.

Step 4. The Purchase Funnel

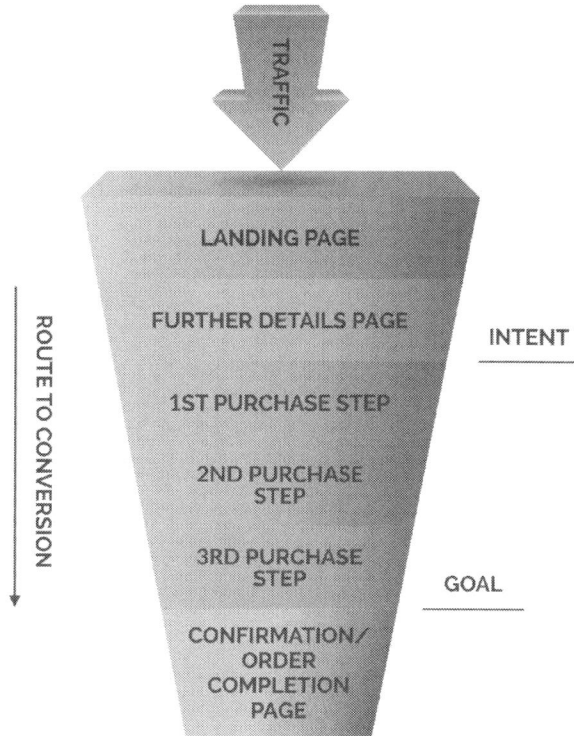

Definition - The process the customer goes through on your website that results in your desired outcome (purchase, click of affiliate link, signup for newsletter, etc.). The funnel is a lot like the buying cycle, only it incorporates just the customer's journey through your specific website.[75]

Keeping with the book example, if you decided to open an ecommerce website selling books and itineraries, each of your customers would progress through a set of steps in order to buy one from you. They would probably begin on your beautifully designed and special offer full underline home page. From there, hopefully they'll browse around, be attracted by your wares, and then move on to a specific product page for whatever books interests them. On this product page they can then research deeper into the book's or trip's contents and pricing. If they're convinced, they will then probably add this book to their cart, arriving at your first checkout page, and might be prompted to create an account. Then they will be prompted to fill out their financial and shipping details on your second checkout page, then on a final purchase confirmation page. Then, after confirming the order, they will be shown the final order completion page that means you just got richer. *This process comprises your purchase funnel.*

Your job is to know and optimise every part of this funnel. You can use one of the many a/b testing services such as Virtual Website Optimiser to help you do this. An a/b test allows you to create alternate versions of each of the pages on your website. In total, 50% of your website visitors will receive the old page, and the other 50% the new test page. You compare which page is more efficient and adopt that one, or continue optimising it again through further rounds of a/b testing.

For example, do more or less people add products to the cart if you make the "buy" button on the product page 10% bigger? Or a brighter hue of red? Or flash every five seconds? Or if you create a promotional offer on the home page that expires in 10 minutes, meaning they have to order now? Do less people leave the checkout process if you remove all external links from its pages? Does showing customer reviews increase or decrease adds to cart? Does letting people buy without creating an account increase the number of people who make it to the confirmation page?

The goal is not to optimise the whole funnel at once, but to identify every single individual step in the funnel, and optimise each in turn—*a* to *b*, *b* to *c*, *c* to *d*, and so on. Because otherwise there will be too many potential variables between a to d, which means you're less likely to get a valid result for your a/b test, or will need a lot of data to do so.

Google Analytics will assist you in creating a funnel for your website. If you find it hard to setup, as you can with any part of the creation of your business, you can just hire someone for a few hours via a service like Upwork to complete it for you.

Step 5. Traffic

Definition - The potential customers that are going to proceed through your purchase funnel.

Now, with everything built and ready for your would-be customers, we just have to target people moving through the buying cycle of your product/service and redirect them into your solution's funnel. This is a fancy way of saying go and find people who want to buy a book about Ghana and redirect them to your home page. There they enter its funnel and hopefully, at the very end of it all, enrich you by making a purchase. Simple as that.

There are many places where you might be able to find people looking planning a holiday to Ghana. In some of those places, you'll have to pay; others will be free. In some, the people will already know they want to buy one. In others, they might just be considering it.

Below is a list of both free and paid sources of traffic. Which you should use will depend a lot on where you are in the buying cycle of your product or service, and what you are selling. Where are your potential customers at each stage of that cycle? Wherever they are is where the adverts for your service need to be.

A: Buying Cycle Stage / B: Where are they likely to be? / C: Attract them to your ecommerce site via:

A: Awareness of Needs / B: Making Google searches for "best guide to Ghana 2016." / C: Blog post on your company blog called "The Definitive List of where to go in Ghana."

A: Assessment of Alternatives / B: Ghana travel sites. / C: Banner adverts on these sites promoting your low-price promise or large range.

A: Alleviation of Risk / B: Create a review site like idealio. / C: Creating an attractive affiliate program, and offering this to the price comparison site to prominently feature you.

A: Decision / B: On your website. / C: An optimised funnel that results in potential customers quickly, and with as few pages and options.

A: Achievement of Results / B: Opening up the package at their door with their new book or itinerary. / C: An advert inside each book you sell offering an incentive to follow you on Facebook to receive future discounts or books.

There are many different sources of traffic for your funnel. Here's a quick overview of the best free and paid options:

Free Traffic Sources

1. SEO

The obvious goal of your site is to rank well in search engines such as Google (Google has such domination at this point that we're really only talking about Google) for relevant search terms such as "travel Ghana" and "Ghana guide." That way you get free, qualified traffic every time someone searches for your products. However, the further you are down the buying cycle, the more competition there will be from competitor websites and services also targeting those valuable purchase-related keywords. Therefore, the harder it will be to get on the first page of Google's results for them.

2. Social Media

The three most well-known options here are Facebook fan pages, a Twitter account, and a company blog. The goal is to acquire friends and followers and entertain them over time, building trust before providing them specific reasons to buy something (new products, sale, coupon codes, etc.). Which platform makes sense depends on what you are trying to sell. If your site has very short-lived promotions, like a flash sale site, writing blog posts about those offers will be redundant since they'll be out of date so fast. In this case, something like Facebook or Twitter would make more sense, where you can quickly broadcast out a short message. If you're selling an ebook about Ghana, however, any kind of blog posts that showcase your knowledge and passion for Ghana are likely to remain relevant for years. You can plug your ebook at the top and bottom of each post. If you don't want to commit to building your own blog, you can go and write "sponsored posts" for other blogs. The Hipstery got more than 50% of its sales from funny guest posts that I'd written on highly trafficked sites. Sometimes, years after those posts had been published, we were still getting 50 people a day to the site and down the funnel because of them. The higher our funnel's conversion rate, the more valuable those 50 visitors became.

Paid Traffic Sources

1. Google Adwords

Google Adwords simply involves buying a place at the top/right of the search results, in the sponsored link boxes. You can specify the exact keywords the user should have entered. As a result, the person who arrives on your site is usually more qualified than via other methods, but the cost of getting that visitor to your site is more expensive. Subtle differences in keywords, such as moving from "Ghana book" to "buy Ghana travel book," can make a surprisingly large difference in your cost per click.

2. Facebook

While Facebook ads have a very low click-through rate (0.5% would already be quite good), if you've an existing fan page, sponsored posts allow your updates to be broadcasted out to more of your fans. This suits certain businesses more than others. Facebook allows a huge amount of targeting about what type of person should see your ad, how old they are, in which city they live, and what interests they have. This is really useful if your product/service has a very clearly defined demographic.

3. Affiliate Program

There are many affiliate marketplaces you can sign up for, such as eJunkie, Zanox, and Commission Junction, but they require an up front free. If you're using Wordpress, you can use a free or nominally priced plugin instead. But like everything, to find good affiliates to promote you on their websites, you'll first need to market your program to them and convince them it's worth their time to market it to their visitors. This is not the low-effort solution many people think it is.

4. Banner Advertising

There are also many marketplaces for this, although so few people click ads it's highly unlikely to be profitable for you. Once you've had banners made for your service (again, you can hire a graphic designer on Upwork for this), you can go to these marketplaces, upload the banners once, and then bid on the advertising spots of relevant websites. The marketplace handles everything else. Some recommended marketplaces are Project Wonderful and Buysellads.

Over time, you should be able develop a conversion rate for each source of traffic. Once you know your average order size and your profit margin, this allows you to place a € price on each visitor via each source of traffic. Keep your paid advertising under than price and you're in the profit zone and growing your business. Really good businesses know that for every €1 they invest in a specific form of advertising, they can track €1.20 (or hopefully much more) flowing through the funnel and into the company's bank account. Once they know this, in theory, they can increase their advertising spend just as much as there is available, relevant traffic to show it to.

Step 6. Outsource, Automate, and Repeat

Definition - Optimise your business processes until they can be completed from anywhere, by anyone.

If you've made it this far, you've already done really well. you now have all of the basic skills to build a simple Internet business. Ideally, you'll know a fair amount about (without being a true expert on) Web design, administration (via Wordpress), Internet marketing, copywriting, customer service, and finance. Name it, and even if you can't do it well, you'll have a good go at it, or find someone who can. The Internet entrepreneur is a jack-of-all-trades and need only be a master in self-promotion. Whether your business becomes your full-time job, or just ticks over some profit, creating some extra pocket money for you, if you've reached this step, you're doing better than most.

But, remember, you got into this to create more time for yourself. I've seen many people build Internet businesses with the goal of becoming "free," only to create businesses that hold them hostage just as much as their previous jobs ever did. They make all the same mistakes I did with the Hipstery. This leaves them stressed out and working more hours for less money than they did in their old jobs. It takes a lot of initial planning to decide how a business should scale, and it's much harder if you wait and try and do it on the fly, once all the business' plates are spinning and you're rushing around trying to stop them all smashing to the ground.

The key to this stage is to track all of the time that you spend on your business—the greater the depth of tracking, the better. You can use apps like Rescue Time for this. This little app tracks where you spend your time and sends you a report each week. Now you know where your time goes. You should begin documenting every business process that you do, starting with those that take the most time. Make the documentation as detailed as possible, and ideally somewhere that's easy to share and update, like a wiki. Get everything that's in your head, out of our head, and into a procedure document.

If you don't do this—and I know this from personal experience—you can start to believe that the business decisions you are making are complicated and specialised, based on some kind of intuitive internal logic that only you have. Only, once you start documenting them, you realise there is no system. You're mostly just making decisions on a whim. By documenting them, you force yourself to create rules for them. From there, it's no problem to hire someone else to do them.

Every few weeks, you should perform an 80/20 analysis on your business. What are the 20% of tasks that take up 80% of your time? Unless a task is absolutely critical, you really like doing it, or it's an utterly irreplaceable core of your business, you should outsource it. The goal is that, within your business, your time is invested in just the things you love doing, or that you do better than anyone else. If a task doesn't fit either of these two categories, hire someone else to do it as soon as you can afford to, either hiring students locally or using remote workers from services like Upwork. The better you get your documentation and the lower the specialism in the task, the less you need to pay to have it completed.

I don't want to be trite in presenting this series of steps, like they are easy, formulaic, or simple, because it is obvious that they aren't. If they were, everyone would have done them already. But they're also far easier than people realise. I've managed to do it, and I'm basically four-fifths of an idiot. The €1250 I invested in the TheTeeDirectory I was able to save fairly quickly because I'd worked for several years while keeping my Freedom Figure low.

While, for some, it's out of necessity, and for others simply from the desire to be their own boss, a whole new generation of micro-entrepreneurs are being created in this way. These are people who are breaking out of the traditional confines of the nine-to-five. They are often quiet, unassuming people that didn't study business or IT—people who never dreamed of being self-employed, but who have tired of trying to find jobs and decided to create one. Their goals are probably not to build a large empire or have employees to manage. They're lifestyle entrepreneurs who just want to be their own bosses, do work that interests them, have a nicer lifestyle, and, if possible, be location-free. These are people finding small problems, developing business hunches, and testing them.

I know each of these steps could be, and in fact often are books in their own right, so you'll have to excuse my brevity when addressing them, since there's more I want to discuss and only so many pages within which to do so. If you'd like to dig deeper into the topics discussed here, I can recommend the following: *The E Myth Revisited* by Michael E. Gerber or if your ambitions are larger and you're thinking startup and then lifestyle business, The *Startup's Owner's Manual* by Paul Blank.

References

Part 1 - Understand

[1] Jeremy Rifkin, *The End of Work - The Decline of the Global Labor Force and the Dawn of the Post-Market Era*, Tarcher/Putnam, New York, 1995.

[2] David Rotman, *How Technology Is Destroying Jobs*, MIT Technology Review, 12.06.2013 (http://www.technologyreview.com/featuredstory/515926/how-technology-is-destroying-jobs/)

[3] Board of Governors of the Federal Reserve System (US), *Industrial Production Index*[INDPRO], Federal Reserve Bank of St. Louis (https://research.stlouisfed.org/fred2/series/INDPRO/)

[4] US. Bureau of Labor Statistics, *All Employees: Manufacturing* [MANEMP], Federal Reserve Bank of St. Louis (https://research.stlouisfed.org/fred2/series/MANEMP/)

[5] Caroline Baum, *So Who's Stealing China's Manufacturing Jobs?*, Bloomberg, 14.10.2003 (http://www.bloomberg.com/apps/news?pid=newsarchive&sid=aRl4bAft7Xw4)

[6] Charles Sizemore, *Will Technology Make Us All Jobless?*, Forbes, 10.11.2013 (http://www.forbes.com/sites/moneybuilder/2013/10/11/will-technology-make-us-all-jobless/)

[7] Ray Kurzweil, The Law of Accelerating Returns, Kurzweil Accelerating Intelligence, 07.03.2001, (http://www.kurzweilai.net/the-law-of-accelerating-

returns)

[8] Anon, Life Expectancy variation over time, Wikipedia, (http://en.wikipedia.org/wiki/Life_expectancy#Life_expectancy_variation_over_time)

[9] Derek Thompson, *The 100-Year March of Technology in 1 Graph*, The Atlantic, 7.4.2012 (http://www.theatlantic.com/technology/archive/2012/04/the-100-year-march-of-technology-in-1-graph/255573/)

[10] Anon, *VW looks to robots to replace retiring boomers*, The Local, 06.10.2014 (http://www.thelocal.de/20141006/vw-says-more-robots-will-replace-retiring-boomers)

[11] George Dvorsky, *How Universal Basic Income Will Save Us From the Robot Uprising*, io9, 31.10.2014 (http://io9.com/how-universal-basic-income-will-save-us-from-the-robot-1653303459)

[12] Bernard Condon und Paul Wiseman, *Millions Of Middle-Class Jobs Killed By Machines In Great Recession's Wake*, Huffington Post Business, 23.01.2013 (http://www.huffingtonpost.com/2013/01/23/middle-class-jobs-machines_n_2532639.html)

[13] Erik Brynjolfsson und Andrew McAfee, *Race against the machine: how the digital revolution is accelerating innovation, driving productivity, and irreversibly transforming employment and the economy*, Lexington, Mass: Digital Frontier Press, 2012

[14] Bernard Condon und Paul Wiseman, *Millions Of Middle-Class Jobs Killed By Machines In Great Recession's Wake*, Huffington Post Business, 23.01.2013

(http://www.huffingtonpost.com/2013/01/23/middle-class-jobs-machines_n_2532639.html)

[15] Sarah Marsh and Holger Hansen, *INSIGHT-The dark side of Germany's jobs miracle*, Reuters, Date 8.2.2012 (http://www.reuters.com/article/2012/02/08/germany-jobs-idUSL5E8D738E20120208)

[16] Anon, *Technology isn't working*, The Economist, 04.10.15 (http://www.economist.com/news/special-report/21621237-digital-revolution-has-yet-fulfil-its-promise-higher-productivity-and-better)

[17] John Brockman, *The Technium: A Conversation With Kevin Kelly*, Edge.org, 2.3.2014 (https://edge.org/conversation/the-technium)

[18] U.S. Senate Committee on Homeland Security & Governmental Affairs, *Exhibit #1a: Offshore Profit Shifting and the U.S. Tax Code - Part 2 (Apple Inc.)*, 21.03.2013 (http://www.hsgac.senate.gov/download/?id=CDE3652B-DA4E-4EE1-B841-AEAD48177DC4)

[19] Vanessa Houlder, *'Dutch sandwich' grows as Google shifts €8.8bn to Bermuda*, Financial Times, 10.10.2013 (http://www.ft.com/intl/cms/s/0/89acc832-31cc-11e3-a16d-00144feab7de.html#axzz3O3LdpWWW)

[20] Karlsson et al, *CEO succession 2007: The Performance Paradox*, Strategy & Leadership, 51: 76-89, 2008 zitiert bei Wulf et al, *Performance over the CEO Lifecycle – A Differentiated Analysis of Short and Long Tenured CEOs*, HHL - Leipzig Graduate School of Management Working Paper No.88, 01.06.2010 (http://www.hhl.de/fileadmin/texte/publikationen/arbeits papiere/hhlap0088.pdf)

[21] Austin Carr, *The Real Story Behind Jeff Bezo's Fire Phone Debacle and what it means for Amazon's Future*, Fast Company, 06.01.2015 (http://www.fastcompany.com/3039887/under-fire)

[22] Jay Greene, *Amazon's tax maneuvers stir up storm in U.K.*, The Seattle Times, 23.08.2014 (http://www.seattletimes.com/special-reports/amazonrsquos-tax-maneuvers-stir-up-storm-in-uk/)

[23] Anon, *Amazon workers in Germany strike again*, Deutsche Welle, 30.05.2014 (http://www.dw.de/amazon-workers-in-germany-strike-again/a-17671569)

[24] Tom Bergin, *Amazon criticized over low German tax bill*, Reuters, 12.07.2013 (http://www.reuters.com/article/2013/07/12/net-us-amazon-germany-tax-idUSBRE96B0HO20130712)

[25] Oliver Wright, *Revealed: Amazon earns more through government grants than it pays in tax*, The Independent, 16.05.2013 (http://www.independent.co.uk/money/tax/revealed-amazon-earns-more-through-government-grants-than-it-pays-in-tax-8617919.html)

[26] Lawrence Latif, *Amazon is criticised over €3m German tax bill*, The Inquirer, 15.07.2013 (http://www.theinquirer.net/inquirer/news/2282344/amazon-is-criticised-over-eur3m-german-tax-bill)

[27] This is, of course, assuming tax is paid by that store to your local government. An oversimplification if you're shopping at a big brand store, which might be using exactly the same tax evasion techniques as Amazon.

[28] Carole Cadwalladr, *My week as an Amazon insider*, The Guardian, 01.12.2013 (http://www.theguardian.com/technology/2013/dec/01/week-amazon-insider-feature-treatment-employees-work)

[29] Oliver Wright, *Revealed: Amazon earns more through government grants than it pays in tax*, The Independent, 16.05.2013 (http://www.independent.co.uk/money/tax/revealed-amazon-earns-more-through-government-grants-than-it-pays-in-tax-8617919.html)

[30] Carole Cadwalladr, *My week as an Amazon insider*, The Guardian, 01.12.2013 (http://www.theguardian.com/technology/2013/dec/01/week-amazon-insider-feature-treatment-employees-work)

[31] Research by the Institute for Local Self-Reliance found that US brick-and-mortar stores require forty-seven people for every $10 million in revenue, Amazon needs just ten. Source - Stacy Mitchell, *The Truth about Amazon and Job Creation*, Institute for Local Self-Reliance, 29,07.2013 (http://www.ilsr.org/amazonfacts/)

[32] Ulrike Dauer, *German Amazon workers on strike*, Market Watch, 22.09.2014 (http://www.marketwatch.com/story/german-amazon-workers-on-strike-2014-09-22-184852716)

[33] Eva Krafczyk, *Poland takes up German slack for Amazon*, Deutsche Welle, 16.12.2014 (http://www.dw.de/poland-takes-up-german-slack-for-amazon/a-18134306)

[34] In 2013, there were 14,000 temporary Amazon workers employed in Germany. Source - 2013 beschäftigte Amazon in Deutschland 14.000 Zeitarbeiter - Sarah Sloat, *Amazon*

Wage Dispute Spreads Beyond Germany, The Wall Street Jornal, 16.12.2013 (http://www.wsj.com/articles/SB10001424052702304173704579262192842185528)

[35] Simon Head, *Mindless: Why Smarter Machines are Making Dumber Humans*, Basic Books, 11.02.2104

[36] Deepa Seetharaman, *Amazon Has Installed 15,000 Warehouse Robots To Deal With Increased Holiday Demand*, Reuters, 01.12.2014 (http://uk.businessinsider.com/r-amazon-rolls-out-kiva-robots-for-holiday-season-onslaught-2014-12?r=US)

Part 2 - Prepare

[37] A research paper about choice found that people with more choices were less likely to buy anything at all, and when they did make a decision, they were less satisfied having picked one from either 24 or 30 choices, as when they had to pick one from just six. I recommend "the paradox of choice" by Barry Schwartz if you want to understand the phenomeon more. Source - Iyengar, S. und M. Lepper. *When Choice Is Demotivating: Can One Desire too Much of a Good Thing? Journal of Personality and Social Psychology* 79 (2000), S. 995-1006. (https://faculty.washington.edu/jdb/345/345%20Articles/Iyengar%20%26%20Lepper%20(2000).pdf)

[38] David McRaney, *You are not so smart.* New York: Gotham Books/Penguin Group, 2011

[39] Ola Svenson, *Are we all less risky and more skillful than our fellow drivers?, Acta Psychologica* 47 (2): 143–148, 1981 (http://heatherlench.com/wp-

content/uploads/2008/07/svenson.pdf)

[40] Patricia Cross, *Not can but will college teachers be improved?*, New Directions for Higher Education 17: 1–15, 1977

[41] Constantine Sedikides et al, *Behind bars but above the bar: Prisoners consider themselves more prosocial than non-prisoners*, British Journal of Social Psychology, (2014)

[42] Cynthia Klein und Marie Helweg-Larsen, *Perceived control and the optimistic bias: A meta-analytic review.* Psychology and Health, 17, 437-446, 18.09.2001 (http://users.dickinson.edu/~helwegm/PDFVersion/Perceived_control_and_the_optimistic.pdf)

[43] Mark Alicke et al, *Personal Contact, Individuation, and the Better-Than-Average Effect*, Journal of Personality and Social Psychology, 01.04.1995 (http://www.researchgate.net/profile/Mark_Alicke/publication/232581252_Personal_contact_individuation_and_the_better-than-average_effect/links/00b49532afd340791b000000)

[44] Amy Crawford, *Why the Best Success Stories Often Begin With Failure*, Smithsonian Magazine, 01.02.2013 (http://www.smithsonianmag.com/innovation/why-the-best-success-stories-often-begin-with-failure-3851517/?no-ist=&inf_contact_key=67d1446d8242439aaeb5040ece423bc570f06d80a668a3329792ee3765da1d0d&page=1)

[45] I don't know the origin of this fable, but I discovered it from entrepreneur and author Derek Sivers - https://sivers.org/horses.

[46] David Heinemyer Hansen, *Ambition Can Be Poision*, Signal vs Noise, 24.06.2013 (https://signalvnoise.com/posts/3547-

ambition-can-be-poison)

[47] Tim Urban, *Why Generation Y Yuppies Are Unhappy*, Huffington Post, 15.11.2013 (http://www.huffingtonpost.com/wait-but-why/generation-y-unhappy_b_3930620.html)

[48] Medvec et al, *When less is more: counterfactual thinking and satisfaction among Olympic medalists,* Journal of Personality and Social Psychology. Oktober 1995;69(4): 603-10.

[49] Daniel Gilbert, Stumbling on happiness. New York: Vintage Books, 2007.

[50] Oliver Burkeman, *This column will change your life: the truth about happiness*, The Guardian, 12.10.2013 (http://www.theguardian.com/lifeandstyle/2013/oct/12/happiness-reality-expectations-oliver-burkeman)

[51] Daniel Gilbert, Stumbling on happiness. New York: Vintage Books, 2007.

[52] Keith Stanovich, *Reconceptualizing Intelligence: Dysrationalia as an Intuition Pump*, Educational Researcher, Mai 1994. 23: 11-21. (http://www.researchgate.net/profile/Keith_Stanovich/publication/240801398_Reconceptualizing_Intelligence_Dysrationalia_as_an_Intuition_Pump/links/540606c50cf2bba34c1e3b7e.pdf).

[53] Josh Kaufman, *The Personal MBA*, Portfolio: Penguin Books, 2010.

[54] Philip Brickman et al, *Lottery Winners and Accident Victims: Is Happiness Relative?*, Journal of Personality and Social Psychology, 1978, Vol. 36, No. 8, 917-927

(http://psy2.ucsd.edu/~nchristenfeld/Happiness_Readings_files/Class%203%20-%20Brickman%201978.pdf)

55 Ed Diener et al, *Beyond the Hedonic Treadmill Revising the Adaptation Theory of Well-Being*, American Psychologist, May–June 2006 (http://www.wisebrain.org/papers/BeyondHedonicTreadmill.pdf)

56 Dimitris Ballas und Danny Dorling, *Measuring the impact of major life events upon happiness*, International Journal of Epidemiology 2007;36:1244–1252 (http://ije.oxfordjournals.org/content/36/6/1244.full.pdf)

57 Nattavudh Powdthavee, *Putting a Price Tag on Friends, Relatives, and Neighbours: Using Surveys of Life Satisfaction to Value Social Relationships*, The Journal of Socio-Economics Volume 37, Issue 4, August 2008, Pages 1459–1480 (http://www.powdthavee.co.uk/resources/valuing_social_relationships_15.04.pdf)

58 Philip Brickman et al, *Lottery Winners and Accident Victims: Is Happiness Relative?*, Journal of Personality and Social Psychology, 1978, Vol. 36, No. 8, 917-927 (http://psy2.ucsd.edu/~nchristenfeld/Happiness_Readings_files/Class%203%20-%20Brickman%201978.pdf)

59 Maria Konnikova, *No Money, No Time*, The New York Times, 13.06.2014 (http://opinionator.blogs.nytimes.com/2014/06/13/no-clocking-out/)

60 Sam Bakkila, *Why You Should Never Have Taken That Prestigious Internship*, Policy.Mic, 14.06.2013 (http://mic.com/articles/48829/why-you-should-never-

have-taken-that-prestigious-internship)

Part 3 - Act

[61] Scott Adams, Scott Adams' Secret of Success: Failure, Wall Street Journal, 16.12.2015 (http://www.wsj.com/articles/SB1000142405270230462610457912 1813075903866)

[62] Jason Roberts, *How To Increase Your Luck Surface Area*, Codus Operandi, 2010 (http://www.codusoperandi.com/posts/increasing-your-luck-surface-area)

[63] Thomas Piketty, *Capital in the Twenty-First Century*, Belknap Press, 01.04.2014, Page. 25.

[64] Matthew Yglesias, *Thomas Piketty doesn't hate capitalism: He just wants to fix it*, Vox.com, 24.04.2014 (http://www.vox.com/2014/4/24/5643780/who-is-thomas-piketty)

[65] Michael Sauga, *The Zombie System: How Capitalism Has Gone Off the Rails*, Spiegel Online International, 23.10.2014 (http://www.spiegel.de/international/business/capitalism-in-crisis-amid-slow-growth-and-growing-inequality-a-998598.html)

[66] Matthew Yglesias, *Thomas Piketty doesn't hate capitalism: He just wants to fix it*, Vox.com, 24.04.2014 (http://www.vox.com/2014/4/24/5643780/who-is-thomas-piketty)

[67] Thomas L. Friedman, *Need a Job? Invent it*, The New York Times, 30.03.2013 (http://www.nytimes.com/2013/03/31/opinion/sunday/fri

edman-need-a-job-invent-it.html)

[68] Meghan Casserly, *The Secret Power Of The Generalist -- And How They'll Rule The Future*, Forbes, 07.10.2012 (http://www.forbes.com/sites/meghancasserly/2012/07/10/the-secret-power-of-the-generalist-and-how-theyll-rule-the-future/)

[69] Vikram Mansharamani, *All Hail the Generalist*, Harvard Business Review, 04.06.2012 (https://hbr.org/2012/06/all-hail-the-generalist/)

[70] Nicole Foster, *Freelancing Advice From 6 Very Successful Designers*, Millo.co (http://millo.co/freelancing-advice-from-successful-designers)

[71] Wendy Kaufman, *A Successful Job Search: It's All About Networking*, National Public Radio (NPR), 03.02.2011 (http://www.npr.org/2011/02/08/133474431/a-successful-job-search-its-all-about-networking)

[72] David Cain, *Most lives are lived by default*, Raptitude.com, 01.07.12 (http://www.raptitude.com/2012/07/most-lives-are-lived-by-default/)

[73] Steve Pavlina, *Let the Old World Collapse*, 08.04.2013 (http://www.stevepavlina.com/blog/2013/04/let-the-old-world-collapse/)

[74] Jack has written an article with detailed advice on passive income on his blog, http://www.jackkinsella.ie/2014/04/24/on-passive-income.html

[75] Could also be a third-party platform where we are selling our product/service. But usually then we won't have access

to optimise all of the purchase funnel and so will have to trust that this platform is doing that well.

Printed in Great Britain
by Amazon